How to Start, Grow an RV Park, RV Resort, or Campground Business

Step-by-Step Guide from Idea to Business Plan to Growth

By

Jack Wendling

Copyrighted Material

Copyright © 2020 – **Valley Of Joy Publishing Press**

All Rights Reserved.

No part of this publication may be reproduced, stored in a retrieval system or transmitted in any form or by any means, electronic, mechanical, photocopying, recording or otherwise without the proper written consent of the copyright holder, except brief quotations used in a review.

Published by:

Valley Of Joy
Publishing Press

Valley Of Joy Publishing Press

Cover & Interior designed

By

Olivia Rothschild

First Edition

Contents

Introduction 9

Why Start an RV Park or Campground? 11

    The Financial Benefits of an RV Park 13

    Other Benefits of Owning an RV Park......................... 14

Types of Parks 17

    RV Campgrounds 17

    RV Parks 18

    RV Resorts 19

    Luxury Camping Resorts 20

What You Need to Get Started 21

    What an RV Park Costs 22

    Location and Land 22

    Utilities 23

    Insurance and Legal Costs 23

    Employees and Maintenance 24

    Marketing and Advertising 25

    Financing an RV Park 25

    Cost of Buying an RV Park... 26

Purchasing an RV Park or Campground 33

    Purchasing an Existing Facility................................... 34

    Building Your Own Facility 34

    Finding an RV Park or Campground for Sale 35

    What to Look for When Buying an RV Park 38

Building an RV Park or Campground 42

    Feasibility Study 43

    Choosing the Land 43

Develop Your Facility 46

    Spacing 48

    Site Type 48

    Ease of Site Access 49

    Traffic Direction and Flow 50

    Road and Site Surface 50

    Level Sites 51

    Utility Connections 51

    Landscaping 52

    Congestion 53

    Security 53

    Build the Park 54

    Franchise Options 54

    Legalities and Utilities 58

    Required Services 61

- Host Campsites 67
- Amenity Considerations 68
  - Should You Have a Clubhouse? 69
  - Renting Out RVs and Cabins 70
  - Additional RV Park Features to Offer 72
  - Top Snacks to Offer 74
- What to Consider in Planning Your Facility 79
  - An Inviting Environment 80
  - Site Spacing 80
  - Friendly Staff 81
  - The RV Site 81
  - Settling In 82
- Pricing, Reservations, and Policies 83
  - Online Reservations 84
  - Determining the Cost for a Site 86
  - Keeping Track of Your Rates 87
  - Setting Up Deposit Rules 88
  - One-Night Stays 89
  - Payment Plan 90
  - 100% Reservation Fee Upfront 91
  - Rules of Conduct 93

Ongoing Operating Costs 95

    Determining Operating Hours 97

    Find Potential Money Makers 101

Identifying and Obtaining Customers 104

Business Essentials 107

    Business Name and Logo 107

    Business Vision/Mission Statement 111

The Business Plan 115

    Executive Summary 116

    Business Structure 118

    SWOT Analysis 125

    Market Analysis 126

    Sales and Marketing Strategy....................................128

    Sources of Income 130

    Generating Startup Capital..133

    Sustainability and Expansion Strategy 134

Other Paperwork Housekeeping 135

    Register as a Legal Entity 136

    Obtain an EIN 137

    Open a Business Bank Account.................................138

    Business License and Permits 142

- Insurance and Bonds 144
  - Common Types of Business Insurance 145
  - Buying Business Insurance 147
- Marketing and Advertising 148
- Employees 154
  - How Many Employees to Hire 155
  - Employee Skills 156
  - The Job Application 157
  - Do You Need an Application? 161
  - Legal Considerations 161
  - How to Conduct Interviews 163
  - Conducting a Job Interview 164
  - Employee Records 168
- Tips and Advice for Being a Good Employer 171
  - Communication 172
  - Flexibility 172
  - Team Building 173
  - Give Feedback 173
  - Know How to Listen 173
  - Foster a Great Experience 174
- Running an RV Park 175

Know the Industry 175

Create a Community 176

Learn the Basics 176

Cleanliness is Important 177

Keep It Simple 177

Do It Right 177

Marketing 178

Adding Facilities 178

Holding Special Events 178

Customer Service 179

Social Media 181

Conclusion 184

Introduction

We are living in a changing world. Financially, the cost of living keeps rising, while wages stay the same. The work-life balance doesn't exist for most as they struggle to maintain the cost of living. If you have found yourself in this situation as I once did, then I want to talk to you about something I discovered. A way that I could relax, enjoy life, have retirement, and own a revenue generating business all at the same time. How is this possible?

The answer lies in looking at what people need. As people retire or as the cost of living rises, people are looking for cheaper ways to get by. One of those popular trends is in downsizing and living smaller. Many are choosing to live on the open road in RVs. Plus, as the baby boomer generation retires, they enjoy the freedom of the open road.

You can enjoy this lifestyle while also starting your own RV park or campground. You'll be providing people with the new trend they want while having your own place to stay. It will be like living and working each day of your life in retirement while enjoying the great outdoors. Let's look into detail at how you can turn this idea into a reality and have a thriving RV park or campground. First, we'll look at why this is a sound business idea, then we'll get into the specifics of how to start your park, and lastly, we'll look at how you can run and maintain it. So let's get started.

Why Start an RV Park or Campground?

At the time of writing this, there are over 13,000 RV parks that are privately owned in the United States. There are also over 1,500 State and National Parks that offer RV sites. These numbers may not seem that impressive, but the fact is that the numbers have been growing and continue to grow. Let's look a little closer at some statistics related to this industry so you can see why it is becoming such a good option for new business owners.

Perhaps the first and most important statistic to consider is the fact that the camping industry, in general, isn't slowing down and doesn't show any signs of doing so anytime soon. In 2018, nearly one million new households became annual campers. Since 2014 the number is about 7 million. Similarly, the number of people who camp for three or more times a year has increased by 72 percent.

Another area of statistics that you want to consider is just what attracts campers. When you can see why people choose to camp, it not only helps you see why starting an RV park is a good business, but it also allows you to determine what type of park you want to start. In 2018, the biggest increase was in the importance of on-site recreation for campers; nearly 40 percent of people selected campgrounds based on on-site recreation. Among these statistics, hiking and canoeing were the most popular outdoor activities with luxury cabin and RV rentals continuing to trend higher than other accommodations.

Another increasing trend is in the age of the individuals camping. The majority of campers in 2018 were millennials who make up over half of the individuals who choose to go camping. In addition, about half of the people who camp have children.

With these numbers, it is easy to see why an RV park can be a good investment. But don't just consider the numbers and take my word for it. Let's consider both the financial and other benefits of starting an RV park before we get into the specifics of starting an RV park.

The Financial Benefits of an RV Park

RV parks are what is considered a very high-yielding investment. This means you can get a ten to twenty percent or more return on your investment. When it comes to real estate asset classes, RV parks are one of the highest-yielding. So if you want a business venture that maximizes the return of your money, then a good place to start is with an RV park.

Also, most RV parks are owned by people like you and me - small owners with little to no debt. These are people who can carry the financing on an RV park. If you get financing at a low interest rate, then it increases the yield you can get on your investment money. In layman's terms, even if an RV park sells at the same return level as other types of real estate, then they would still overcome the competition based on seller carry.

It is also important to state here that most sellers carry financing and don't need a credit review from a loan committee. This means that even if you have bad credit, you can still get a seller carry loan. Most seller carry loans are also "non-recourse" in nature. This means that even if you default on a loan and sell your property at a loss, the note holder still can't come after you personally for any deficiency.

Other Benefits of Owning an RV Park

As someone who runs an RV park, I must tell you it is so much fun; I would do it for free. While I wouldn't suggest you go this far, it doesn't mean that owning an RV park is a very appealing business venture. There are a few other business ventures where you can dedicate your days to having fun. Consider three main benefits you get from owning an RV park.

First, you get to offer people a wonderful vacation experience away from home. People who visit RV parks or campgrounds often turn to the owners for support and guidance when it comes to having a great vacation experience. You'll be expected to talk about the local things you do and make appropriate recommendations. Your guests may also want you to help show them how to hook up utilities and do other daily tasks if they are new to the RV experience. Often just a pleasant greeting is all people need to have a good experience at your park.

Second, when you own an RV, you get to be outdoors and fixing things on a regular basis. This is especially true is you want to be a hands-on RV park owner; there will always be things for you to fix or improve. You'll need to be a jack-of-all-trades to work on a variety of things. Even if you have the staff to help you make repairs and improvements, you'll still need to be good at multitasking.

Lastly, you need to be prepared that you're the boss. This means that all problems end with you, and all decisions are yours. You get to determine who to give a discount to, what advertising to use and what to upgrade. When you are the boss, it gives you great freedom to set your schedule and run your park as you see fit, but it also means great responsibility since every decision you make will impact the success of your park.

Perhaps a side benefit to consider that may or may not apply to you is the future an RV park can offer. When you own an RV park, you are essentially creating an estate that both you and your future generations can enjoy and benefit from. While many dwindle their savings after retirement, an RV park can not only enjoy their retirement but can also have cash flow each day. You are actually building on an asset that your future generations can benefit from. Successful RV parks are easily worth over a million dollars.

It is clear that owning an RV park is a great investment. It provides you with both financial and non-financial benefits. So if you are interested in continuing this unique opportunity, then the next thing you need to do is decide what type of RV park you want to open. Let's consider the options available to you.

Types of Parks

When it comes to RV parks and campgrounds, there are four main types you need to consider: campgrounds, parks, resorts, and luxury camping. Each option offers its own benefits and operational considerations. Let's do a brief comparison of the three main options: a campground, park, and resort.

RV Campgrounds

The type of people who choose to stay at RV campgrounds often prefer the beauty and relaxation of the atmosphere in which the park is set over the benefits of modern amenities.

RV campgrounds are often located in more rustic areas near national parks and forests or areas where there are plenty of outdoor activities to be had.

If you choose to own an RV campground, you will often price your sites lower than an RV park or resort. The trade-off is that you aren't expected to provide as many amenities. Often a fire pit and/or picnic table with a public bathroom and communal shower is all that people expect to get from a primitive RV campsite. Although you can choose to offer more and some RV campgrounds will have electric and sometimes water. It is very rare to find sewer connections, but most campgrounds will have a fresh water tap and dumping station.

RV Parks

This is basically the middle ground option. It is one of the more common options when it comes to starting an RV park. Often they will feature some of the more common amenities, but often you'll offer the sites at a lower price than a resort. Your customers will expect the sites to have electric hookups at 30-50 amp, water, and often access to the sewer. You'll need to be prepared to accommodate both overnight and extended stay guests. Popular amenities that guests look for when choosing RV parks include on-site laundry, free internet, and sometimes cable television hookups.

If you choose this option, then you'll need to realize that setting the price of your RV park is often determined by how close you are to nearby attractions. RV parks can charge more if they are located near amusement parks or recreational activities. Also, the size of your sites and ease of access will impact how much you can charge and the number of customers that will come to your park.

RV Resorts

As the name suggests, this is the most deluxe and luxurious option you can provide your customers. These parks typically offer full hookups for all sizes and types of RVs. They often offer amenities similar to hotels, offering things like clubhouses, fitness centers, convenience stores and/or restaurants along with common amenities such as laundry and internet. Many resorts also offer on-site recreation and entertainment such as swimming pools and tennis courts. RV resorts often place a focus on the longer-term resident but will also see seasonal residents as well. You can often charge the highest for these sites but will need to pay more to set up your resort and maintain it.

A more recent option that many are considering is luxury camping resorts that offer glamping. This is one thing to consider as it is a new middle ground between a campground and an RV resort.

Luxury Camping Resorts

Glamping is an option that prevents your customers with the chance to enjoy the beauty of nature in a modern and luxurious experience. Your focus is to allow your customers to experience unique outdoor experiences while still being able to enjoy all the comforts of modern society.

Glamping is about more than simply providing your guests with a nice tent. Rather it is about showcasing a unique destination while offering advantages your guests can't get anywhere else. Stay in a yurt at the top of a mountain. Enjoy a forest canopy from a treehouse. Relax in an eco-lodge while taking in panoramic views. These are just a few of the options. If you know of a unique location or your park has something unique to offer, then consider capitalizing on it by offering a glamping experience for those who want to get out of their RV for a little while.

No matter which of these options you choose, the basics of what you need to get started and the business aspect are all going to be about the same. The only time there will be a difference is when it comes to building and designing your park. The type of park you choose will also determine the type and style of marketing you choose to do once you get started. So let's take a look at what you need to get started with your RV park.

What You Need to Get Started

When it comes to getting started with your RV park, there are two major steps you need to make at the beginning. The first is to consider the financial aspect of starting a park. How much will it cost you to start? What are your financing options? Once you have the necessary finances needed to get started, then you can start looking into the second aspect, which is where your park will be located and how to find a suitable place to locate your park. Let's consider both of these areas in greater detail.

What an RV Park Costs

Before you can start considering the financial options for starting your RV park, you need to consider a breakdown of how much it costs to start an RV park and understand just where your money is going. Most aspects of an RV park startup cost will vary based on where you plan to have your park, whether you plan to build or buy an existing park, and exactly what you need to do to get up and running. I'll break down the costs for you based on the park I started so you can at least have a general idea for how much it will cost you.

Location and Land

As we will discuss in a moment, the biggest part of owning and operating an RV park comes down to the location of your park and how much land you need to purchase. RVs can take up a lot of space, and even just shooting for 30-50 long term campers at a time can take up a lot of room.

Depending on the acreage you are looking for, and where you plan to place your RV park, the cost for the land can range from $15,000 to $50,000. This can be the biggest and scariest number when it comes to considering the startup costs for your RV park. We'll look more at how much space you need in a moment. However, it is always a good idea to shop around in your area and see if you can find a cheap option for buying a large property.

Utilities

This can vary depending on what type of park you choose to build. As we discussed, if you plan to just open a rustic campground, then you won't have to do much in the way of utility hookups. I chose to set up a standard RV park, so I needed to provide fresh water, electricity, internet, and cable hookups for all my sites.

If you purchase an RV park that is already in operation, you may already have these hookups in place. If you choose to build a new RV park, then you'll want to take into account the cost of installing hookups, and this can sometimes cost more than the land itself.

Let's again assume that you are looking to have 30 to 50 sites, and you want the minimum hookups for an RV park such as water, electricity, and internet. At a minimum, this could be $5,000 per site for hookups.

Insurance and Legal Costs

In order to start an RV park, you need to take care of the business aspect and establish yourself as a business in the form of an LLC or corporation. You will also need to make sure you purchase the appropriate level of insurance and have all the appropriate zoning and regulation permits. If you aren't up on business and legal issues, you may want to consider the cost of hiring a legal attorney. While the costs of filing city and county permits can be costly, it will be cheaper than paying the fine for violating zoning laws or forgetting a crucial business license. It is important that you cover all your legal aspects, we'll discuss more on this later.

Employees and Maintenance

Once you have your land purchased and the hookups and business aspects covered, you still have a few other costs to consider. You'll need to consider the cost of hiring employees and keeping up your park. If you have a small park, you may be able to do several tasks on your own to keep costs down at first. However, with time and as you grow, you may want to consider hiring employees to help.

Whether you start out with employees or just try it on your own, you should always consider the costs of upkeep for your park. You'll need to maintain footpaths, upkeep landscape, so everything looks inviting to your guests, maintaining any facilities and amenities as well as manning the welcome center to check guests in and out during their stays.

Marketing and Advertising

Another part of running your business that contributes to overall costs is marketing and advertising. Even if you only focus on local media at first, you can easily spend hundreds of dollars. You can cut some costs if you are comfortable using social media like Facebook and Instagram. We'll discuss more about marketing and advertising efforts later in this book.

Now that you kind of have an idea of how much it will cost you to start your RV park, we need to consider what your financing options are and how you can get the necessary funds to start your RV park.

Financing an RV Park

The cost of starting your RV park can vary greatly when considering the factors above. When it comes to helping you with these funds, there are two main options for financing your new RV park.

Commercial Loans

This is a loan that is often taken out by an individual on behalf of the business. It is often used to provide the needed funds to develop and grow a business. It is often secured by some form of property or asset.

Unsecured, Fixed-Term Business Loan

This can be a better option if you are starting a less expensive RV park. The lender gives you the amount you need, and you agree to pay a specific amount over a specific time period. There are a few things to consider when deciding what type of loan is right for your needs.

Cost of Buying an RV Park

The price you'll pay to purchase or build an RV park varies. Will you buy the land and the business, will you buy the business and lease the land or will you buy the land and start the business from scratch? Often a smaller RV park in a less popular area can cost you as little as $300,000 while a successful RV park in a popular area can easily cost $1 million.

Some factors to keep in mind when purchasing an RV park include the following:

- The amount of your down payment.

- The size and location of the property.

- Projected annual business earnings.

- Accommodation options, including cabins or tent areas along with RV sites.

- Guest facilities, such as tennis courts, swimming pools, playgrounds, and clubhouses.

- Projected occupancy rate and/or frequency of return customers.

- Planned number of staff and their potential experience and qualifications.

- Current market conditions, including any competition from other nearby accommodation providers.

These are just a few of the main factors. It is very complicated when it comes to valuing a business. Other than the purchase price of the property or the existing RV park, you'll need to also factor in the cost for any improvements, repairs, or building that you'll need to do right away. It can be a good idea to talk with an accountant or business adviser in order to make sure you are paying a fair price for the land or existing RV park.

Business Factors to Consider

Purchasing or building an RV park is a big investment, so you need to consider several financial factors before making the decision to seek financial assistance with the purchase process.

First, consider your level of experience. If you have any experience with managing a place of accommodation such as a campground, hotel, or other vacation location, this can increase your chance of a successful loan application. Experience can also increase your chances of having a profitable business.

Another thing to consider is your qualifications. Do you have a degree in hotel or hospitality management? Do you have any education or experience in business? These qualifications can help you with owning and managing an RV park. It can also help strengthen your chance of getting approved for a loan application.

Third, having the required licenses and permits. Depending on the type of RV park you plan to purchase or build, you'll need the appropriate licenses and permits from agencies such as the Department of Environmental Protection or the Department of Revenue. We'll discuss more about these licenses and permits later. While the requirements will vary by state, county, or city, you may want to contact a commercial property lawyer to make sure you have everything you need. This will also make the loan application a lot easier.

You should also know and consider potential occupancy levels. If you're purchasing an existing RV park, consider the numbers on how full or empty the park has been during peak season. Occupancy levels change often and are often impacted by location and season. However, as a general rule, any occupancy rate below 50% will indicate an underperforming business.

Lastly, consider the number of annual stays. The key to nearly any business is that of return customers. Those who are annual site holders can impact the financial stability of an RV park or campground. If you are purchasing an existing RV park, then you should look for one with a decent number of annual site holders.

Is the Business Worth Buying

If you plan to buy an existing RV park, you need to make sure you are making a worthwhile financial purchase. To do this, you want to consider the business' finances. To do this, consider the following:

First, consider current business finances. Ask yourself the following:

- What is the recurring net operating revenue?

- How has the business performed in the last five years?

- Are there areas where the park can be improved and/or grow?

If you are buying an RV park as an investment, it is important that you also consider the financial stability of the people staying there as well.

It is also a good idea to consider why the current owners are selling. Are they looking for a profit, or is there a more worrisome reason that they want to sell the park?

Third, look at the occupancy levels. A lender is often going to want to see proof that an RV park or campground has high occupancy levels before they approve a loan application. In addition to providing the lender with year-round occupancy levels, you should also provide the ratio of annual site holders. This will give both the lender and yourself an idea of where the business strengths are and where things can be improved.

You also need to consider the location of the park. Consider both the proximity to local attractions and the competition of other places where people can seek accommodations. Is there something about the park you are considering that makes it stand out from the competition? If it doesn't stand out, then be sure you consider how much financing it will take to improve the park and make it different from the competition.

Also, take the time to consider the facilities. Ask yourself the following:

- Are there the necessary facilities for the type of guests you'll be attracting?

- Are there other recreational opportunities in the nearby area?

Sixth, make sure you have the necessary building and pest reports. No one is going to stay at a park that has pest problems, and being in nature can make these more difficult to control. The cost of pest control can also be a big deal for financing. So make sure you inquire about any issues and/or renovations that need to be made before taking over a property. It might help you to negotiate a lower selling price or tell you that you need to ask the lender for additional funds.

You'll also want to consider terms if you aren't going to buy the property. It is best to look for a long lease term so you will have enough time to grow your business and pay off your initial loan. Unless you are knowledgeable on the subject, it can be a good idea to have a lawyer look through the lease agreement, so you understand all the rights and responsibilities when it comes to maintenance and upkeep of the property.

Lastly, you want to consider any local restrictions. If you are going to need to renovate or upgrade the park after purchase, then you'll want to check in with local government agencies to see if there are any restrictions on the improvements you can make. This may influence how much it costs and impact how much you need to ask the lender for.

Getting or building an RV park is a great way to have a steady income and start a business, but the cost can vary greatly. Once you have a down payment ready and have found the right option for you, then you can start looking for the right business loan that will help you finance your dreams. Let's look a little closer at the purchase process, depending on whether you want to buy an existing park or build your own, plus a third option of franchising.

Purchasing an RV Park or Campground

Perhaps the easiest way to invest in an RV park or campground is to buy one that already exists, but there are other options if there isn't one for sale in your area. You can own an RV park or campground either by buying an existing facility, build your own, or invest in a franchise. As RV sales increase, there is a greater demand for these facilities, so now is the time to decide which option is best for you and to pursue it. We'll look at franchising in a moment, but first, we are going to focus on the first two options.

Purchasing an Existing Facility

There are both pros and cons of buying an existing RV park or campground. You'll already have a business infrastructure in place, along with all the necessary permits and land development. However, you will also be inheriting the previous owner's reputation and marketing with the purchase, either good or bad. This needs to be carefully considered in your business plan since this can be very hard to reverse if it is bad. You may also end up purchasing a facility that needs upgrades in order to compete with newer parks in your area. This would be another financial impact on the startup costs of your new park or campground.

Building Your Own Facility

Purchasing land and building your own RV park or campground can be quite the task. You'll need to get all the required permits and design all the infrastructure, such as road systems, electrical lines, water lines, and sewer service. However, when building your facility, you can plan for deficiencies and overcome them before they become an issue for your guests. You also have the opportunity to design a new park with all the modern amenities that guests will prefer over other nearby accommodations. Let's look at both of these options in greater detail to help you make the right decision on how to get started.

Finding an RV Park or Campground for Sale

I can tell you from personal experience that buying an RV park is more than an investment; it is a lifestyle. It is a great way to combine the concept of your retirement and investment in one package and enjoy the benefits of both. RV parks give you a high investment return while enjoying a satisfying lifestyle. You can be your own boss in a beautiful scenic area while working with happy people and spending a lot of your time outside; for most, this is the dream. The first step in purchasing an existing facility is to find an RV park or campground for sale. There are more options available to you than you may think.

The Internet

There are hundreds of RV parks or campgrounds for sale at any time, and most of them can be viewed from the comfort of your living room. If you have computer access, go on the internet and take a look at the number of parks you can consider. The most popular option is the website www.rvparkstore.com. Here you'll find hundreds of parks along with their locations and basic facts. The internet allows you to see a number of properties and compare deals easily. It is also a great way to define the specifics you want in a park, whether for your budget or interests.

Direct Mail

Once you know of the specific area where you want to purchase your RV park or campground, you can send postcards or letters to RV parks in that area. You will often be surprised at how many people respond to these direct mailings. It may vary depending on why the owners want to sell, but you may find a great option before it is listed for others to consider. Even if a park owner isn't interested in selling, they may know of someone who is interested.

Cold Calling

This is a great alternative to direct mailing. Call the owners of RV parks in places you are interested in and see if they are interested in selling. This may sound scary at first, but you aren't trying to sell them anything. You'll find that most people are actually quite pleasant and willing to talk with you. Even if they don't want to sell, they can give you a great deal of information on owning and operating an RV park. So you'll be sure to get something from the call.

Brokers

As you start to look at listings online, you'll notice that there are a small number of brokers who deal in RV parks or campgrounds exclusively. You can call these brokers to see if they have any properties that meet your specific criteria. You will notice that most brokers focus on a specific geographic area and may have sellers that don't list their facilities for sale on public sites. This means that finding a broker is often one of the best ways to find the best facility for you to purchase. You can also negotiate better through a broker since they want to pay for their commission.

Word-of-Mouth

If you spend your time talking to other RV park owners, then word will eventually get out that you are looking to purchase a facility in a specific area. This will set off a chain reaction since it is a small community and people talk. Whether it is a park owner, a broker, or a banker, you'll be surprised by what they offer you.

RV parks are a great investment, and there are plenty available to purchase. You just need to know where to look and be diligent in your search. Through a combination of the above, you are sure to find plenty of listings to consider in a short amount of time. Once you have found a few options that work for you, then you can move on to consider each park. Let's look at what you should consider before purchasing a facility.

What to Look for When Buying an RV Park

If you choose to buy an existing RV park or campground, then there are a few things you want to consider and look for when choosing what to purchase. Let's look at the specifics of what you should seek out when buying an existing facility.

The Location

Real estate is all about location, and this is even truer when it comes to the hospitality industry. Occupancy levels are nearly completely dependent on the area where your business operates. If possible, you should look to purchase an existing facility that is close to interstates or other heavy traffic flow areas. It is also good if you can find an existing facility that is near to popular landmarks, so you have an additional attraction for visitors from all over the world.

Amenities and Services

An RV park needs to provide travelers with the services they can't get while traveling on the road. This means you want to look for an existing facility that already has clean amenities and functioning services such as drinking water connections, a sewer system, and the internet. You may want to consider putting more money into purchasing a park that has added amenities such as a gas station, a restaurant, and recreational activities in order to increase the popularity and potential revenue of your facility.

Online Presence

Nearly 93 percent of consumers use online reviews to make decisions about where they will spend their money. Before purchasing an existing facility, it is a good idea to check the park's online reputation. You should ideally buy a facility that already has positive online reviews, a strong social media presence, and a fully-functional website.

If an existing facility meets these three main criteria, the next step you need to do is dig a little deeper. Choosing an RV park is about more than what you simply see. Make sure you do your due diligence before you begin the process of purchasing an existing facility. Let's consider the additional homework you should do first.

In the United States, there are typical business licenses needed to run a business, but there are also industry-specific ones that need to be considered as well. For example, the Department of Environmental Protection supervises RV parks and campgrounds for their environmental footprint. Before purchasing an existing facility, you need to make sure that all their paperwork is in order and that they meet all regulations related to all required permits.

You don't want to purchase an existing facility only to find yourself in a legal dispute, so make sure you are aware of any zoning restrictions or environmental protection laws in the area where you are purchasing. It is a good idea to also consider any restrictions or laws that are soon to go into place. This can give you a good idea of how much you can expand or add amenities in the future.

It is also a good idea to have the property inspected just as you would with a home purchase. An RV park is primarily affected by external threats like rodents and weather conditions. It is best to have the property checked for infestations and pests along with the durability of any buildings.

Whenever you are purchasing an existing business, it is important to consider the projected revenue. Take the time to do some calculations to see not only the cost of running the business but also to determine the expected income of the property. To do this, you need to consider the occupancy rate and the capacity for the facility. Remember that RV parks or campgrounds can have seasonal variations. So get forecast variations for income in both peak periods and during the offseason.

Lastly, keep in mind that as an RV park owner, your main responsibility is to provide traveling guests with services.

Consider all the needed systems of your guests and how close they are to the facility you are thinking of purchasing. This means things like road systems, electrical lines, water lines, and sewer systems. If these aren't available, then you won't be able to offer the facilities that customers will seek in an RV park or campground.

Once you have found a suitable existing facility to purchase, you can move on in the process. This would be to get a loan needed to purchase the property and then take over the operation of the business. Of course, there is also the option of building your own RV park or campground. This presents a different set of criteria and considerations.

Building an RV Park or Campground

When you choose to build your own RV park or campground from scratch, then you have a new set of things to consider. How do you design your facility? Where do you plan to build? What should you consider before starting? There are five main steps to take to help you design and build the best RV park or campground.

Feasibility Study

The first thing you want to do when building a park is to complete a comprehensive feasibility study. In this study, you want to have a written description of the type of park that best for the market you are selecting along with a projected profit and loss for the first five years your park is in operation.

At this point, you may have identified a specific property, or you may only have a general area in mind. The feasibility study can help you make a decision on whether or not to purchase a franchise or operate as an independent park once you build the park. We'll discuss more about choosing a franchise in a moment.

Choosing the Land

The second step is to identify the specific parcel of land where you will develop your park. After this, you need to start quantifying costs linked to the specific parcel of land.

Before you commit to purchasing the land, you'll want to ask yourself the following questions:

- Are you able to get the appropriate zoning?

- What improvements are needed?

- How is sewage handled?

- Where does your water come from?

- Are there any specific environmental requirements?

- Are there any drainage issues?

- How level is the land, and is it too steep to be developed?

- Is there room to build cabins or other fixed rental units?

Perhaps the biggest question when it comes to choosing a location for your RV park or campground is how many acres you need to purchase? As a general rule of thumb, you should have no less than 10 sites per acre. In some areas, this number of sites may be limited to 10 to 15. Some permit requirements will also give minimum measurements of how wide and long each site needs to be.

When it comes to deciding how many sites your park will have, keep in mind larger motorhomes and fifth wheels. Some can be as long as 40 feet and have multiple slide-outs to make room for. Ensure there is enough room between campsites to fit the largest lengths and widths of these rigs.

The goal is to make sure your guests have enough space to enjoy their experience without feeling like they are on top of the other guests. Also, make sure you have room for landscaping options such as fire pits that could increase the appeal and benefit your RV park.

Develop Your Facility

Once you have your land ready, then you can develop your specific RV park or campground. This includes planning the layout of sites and amenities. If you choose to purchase a franchise, this process will be done for you. If you are building an independent park, then you may want to hire someone to design the park, unless you are comfortable doing it yourself.

Initially, you want to do a preliminary concept design to help you obtain the proper zoning and planning department approval. Don't put a lot of effort into detailed plans until you have approval on the preliminary concept design. If you are going to seek help, make sure it is a local designer or engineer with knowledge of RV park businesses. This ensures they know proper design as well as the zoning and licensing requirements for your area. If you plan to try your own preliminary plan, then be sure to keep the following in mind when designing an RV park.

The design of an RV park is impacted by several things, including a suitable location, the characteristics of the target market, any potential obstacles and related restrictions, any limits imposed by permits, and the analysis of the most suitable type of park. Since every RV facility is unique, there is no specific layout that works for an RV park or campground. The biggest trade-off you need to consider is the size of each site and the total number of spaces at your facility.

An RV park focuses on the RV traveler can range from a dense level of site spacing with narrow interior roads to generously spaced sites and wide interior loads. This can also make the difference between how much land you need to purchase as well as how many sites you can put on the land. Of course, this will also have an impact on your daily rate.

In addition, your park design needs to take into consideration the new and longer "big rigs" that also have slide rooms on both sides. In order to classify yourself as "big rig friendly," you need to provide appropriately sized sites of length and width to attract this high revenue traffic.

However, this doesn't mean that all sites in your park need to accommodate these larger rigs; unless it is needed to cover the projected needs of your target client base. Keep in mind that "big rig friendly" doesn't just apply to site size, but also means the width of interior roads, the ease of turning, and the lack of obstructions. Overhead clearance can be another factor when it comes to tree limbs.

Let us now consider some of the primary categories and concerns that you need to analyze and consider when developing a preliminary design plan for your RV park or campground.

Spacing

We've kind of already discussed this above when talking about "big rig friendly." However, when it comes to specific numbers, the absolute minimum spacing is about 25 feet in width. The "comfort" zone starts around 27 to 28 feet, and often 30 to 35 feet gives guests a sense of openness. Length can vary based on the size of the RV, but to attract the larger rigs, a length of about 75 feet is often required.

Site Type

Most guests prefer pull-through sites rather than back-in sites; however, they are less "efficient" when it comes to space utilization. Many who are only staying overnight consider the pull-through site essential. Some RV travelers may not be confident about backing into a site or don't want the hassle of unhitching a tow car. This isn't to say a park can't survive by offering only back-in sites, but you will also lose some business if you don't offer some pull-through sites.

Ease of Site Access

When offering back-in sites, they can be made easier for RVs to access if you take a few considerations in the basic layout. A site that is at an angle to the roadway eliminates the need to make a sharp turn. Also, a roadway that is wide enough to accommodate a longer rig's turning radius will make the sites seem "friendlier" to the RV driver. The interior road design should also allow the vehicle to back in the direction of the driver's side rather than the other direction. This is to help the driver see the back of the RV in relation to the site as they maneuver during the backup process. Lastly, sites should be free of any overhead or side obstructions. Even pull-through sites should be free of these obstructions as well. If obstructions prevent people from completely pulling through or backing out easily, then they may view this as an inconvenience.

Traffic Direction and Flow

Just as when planning a city, the flow of traffic in an RV park or campground can have both positive and negative consequences that need to be evaluated when determining the layout of a facility. The objective is to distribute traffic as evenly as you can in order to minimize congestion and its impact on your guests. One way traffic can often be helpful, but the streets need to be wide enough to allow larger rigs to make easy turns. A general rule of thumb is that 25 foot wide one-way roads are appropriate. If there are two-way roads on interior roads, then they need to be wide enough to allow for large rigs passing each other in opposite directions. About 30 feet width is appropriate. Keep in mind the amount of traffic impact when designing a park as well; guests won't want to be close to an entrance if it sees a disproportionate amount of traffic.

Road and Site Surface

While you have a range of options when it comes to road types and site surfaces, the better the grade of the surface, the happier your guests will be. Most directories described interior roadways as paved, gravel, or dirt. Most RVers prefer paved interior roads, but will also take graded interior gravel roads as a minimum. Many RVers will avoid dirt roads, particularly in areas where it rains regularly. Commonly you will see gravel parking pads with concrete patios. In damp climates, high-grade gravel with appropriate drainage is often as effective as having a paved site with puddles.

Level Sites

This is an often-overlooked characteristic of RV parks but is often taken seriously by RVers. Most RVs don't have an onboard system to help level an RV. If a site is not level, then RVers need to use blocks and go through a series of trial-and-error attempts to make their living space comfortable. Even RVs with air level systems are limited in how much of a slope they can compensate for before resorting to blocks as well. However, during the construction phase of a new park, it is relatively easy to accomplish level sites, and this can make your guests want to return.

Utility Connections

RVs always have utilities on the driver's side and near the back third of the RV. The typical water hose is 25 feet in length. The average electrical cord is about the same length. A sewer hose is either 10 or 20 feet in length, but often only stretch to about 80% of that length. It is important to know these numbers since you should always put utilities where most RVs can easily reach them. Proper placement of utilities means more than the simple horizontal distance, but also refers to vertical distance as well. Make sure your hookups aren't placed in unnecessarily tall spots or too close to the side of the rig where slide-out rooms or doors are blocked.

Landscaping

The best RV parks or campgrounds are ones that provide their guests with the feeling of a private "space." Otherwise, guests will feel like they are simply staying in a parking lot. No matter how small of a space, RVers want to take "ownership" of their space. It is important that you somehow define an RV space by more than simple striping on the blacktop. Consider something like privacy fencing; it won't block visual access to the site but will provide a sense of a "private place." You can also do this with trees and shrubs for a more natural feel, but ensure they aren't obtrusive to the navigation of the site. Landscaping can range from simple to elaborate, with plenty of variations in between. The best form of landscaping is one that takes advantage of the natural setting of the park and blends in with the surrounding area while still providing a level of separation and privacy from other guests.

Congestion

When observing a good design layout, don't forget to consider where a tow car or towing vehicle is going to be parked. If there isn't room at the site for a towed vehicle and no designated nearby parking, then the vehicle will end up on the street. If your park becomes full, so will the streets. This causes the streets to become more narrow and potentially hazardous to navigate. So avoid congestion by making sure your park layout provides ample room for parking all manner of vehicles.

Security

In recent years, the concern about security among RVers has increased. If a park doesn't feel safe and secure, then this will likely impact the occupancy rate. In the future, security is likely to have a big impact on RV parks. Often an RV park in a more urban area is going to have more concerns than a park in a more remote area. In some situations, fencing and a gated entrance may be needed. Less populated areas will need less security, but it can't be ignored entirely. Some park locations will have natural barriers like a shoreline or other topographical features. This needs to be considered when planning security requirements for your park. Whatever level of security is needed, the RV guest needs to have a sense that the management has recognized the importance of a secure location and is taking steps to provide it.

Build the Park

Once you use this preliminary plan to get zoning and planning department approval, you can hire a local engineer or architect to draw up final plans and start getting bids for construction. Then you can begin construction on the park. While construction is being done, this can be a great time to work on the marketing and business plans to help with the operation of the park once construction is finished.

If neither purchasing an existing park or building your own sounds like options for you, then the last thing you should consider is franchise options. Let's consider how this can be a different option and what makes it different from operating an independent campground. Plus, we'll look at a few of the main franchise options available.

Franchise Options

When building an RV park or campground from scratch, then you can choose to focus on a franchise or an independent campground. Neither option has more pros over the other, it really just comes down to what your goals are for operating an RV park or campground.

The two largest franchises in the United States is KOA and Yogi Bear's Jellystone Park. Both have a solid reputation for being family-friendly and are often found in the Top 50 Franchises list published by the Franchise Business Review. Franchises must meet certain quality standards and are routinely inspected. With a franchise, you also have the benefit of an existing infrastructure when it comes to brand recognition, reservations, and marketing. If you choose to join a franchise, you'll often need to do four things:

1. Get location approval to ensure it doesn't conflict with other franchise campgrounds.

2. Submit an application.

3. Sign a business contract and develop a marketing plan that matches the franchise.

4. Undergo some level of training on how to operate your facility as a part of a franchise.

Franchises provide you with the support you need and brand name behind you, while independent campgrounds give you more flexibility in operation and making it your own. To help you make a decision, let's consider the two most common franchises and what they have to offer you.

Yogi Bear Jellystone Parks

When it comes to franchising with Yogi Bear, the numbers speak for themselves. Owned by Leisure Systems Inc. (LSI), they have been ranked for exceptional performance in several areas, including financial strength and stability, growth rate, and brand power. In 2016, LSI sales totaled $108 million. At the same time, the average park revenue was $1.45 million, and the top five Jellystone Parks grossed an average of $4.7 million. Consider just a few stats that the company posted in 2016:

- Revenues went up 11.6 percent in the first 10 months.

- Overall occupancy nights were up 12.8 percent.

- 42 percent of Jellystone Parks had a double-digit increase in revenue.

- Store revenues were up 6.5 percent, and ancillary revenue was up 6.1 percent.

How these numbers translate into money for you has to do with how the franchise operates. LSI used the Base Business Exclusion (BBE), which calculates the operating royalty on the increase in business. This means LSI wants you to grow your business because it makes money for the company. The BBE is determined from your gross sales in the year prior to joining the franchise. You only pay operating royalties on the gross sales above the BBE that comes from using the Jellystone Park brand.

The Jellystone Park franchise also offers stability. Originally founded in 1969, the company continues to thrive. The original location in Sturgeon Bay, Wisconsin, still exists, and the franchise has now grown to 31 states and four provinces. Even during economically challenging times, the franchise has continued to grow in both revenue and locations. During the 2006-2011 recession, the average revenue per park increased by 10 percent, and the locations grew from 65 to 77.

Jellystone Park is also a franchise that is focused entirely on the family demographic. Other organizations have only recently started to recognize the benefits of marketing towards families, while LSI has been doing it for almost 50 years. So if you choose this franchise, you'll be a part of a special niche that you won't find elsewhere in the RV and camping industry. In addition to this, you are given proven, comprehensive, and proprietary training. You'll also have operational and marketing support to help you succeed. You can also have access to store sales with a line of quality and unique licensed merchandise. All this while you enjoy your independence as an entrepreneur.

KOA

KOA is another franchise that has designed, developed, and operated campground for over 50 years. Their focus is on increasing the strength and size of the KOA franchise. In addition to offering you consultation, they will also partner with you to make your RV campground a success. KOAs offer people the full range of camping experiences and are able to grow and change in order to meet the future demands of RV camping. Just keep in mind that when joining the KOA franchise, they don't purchase the land, finance the construction or build the campground for you.

Now that you have an idea of what type of park or campground you want to focus on, let's consider more of the specifics involved. The first thing you should consider is the legalities of the process and how to ensure you meet all of the legal requirements to open an RV park or campground.

Legalities and Utilities

As with any business, when you are first getting started, there are legal considerations. With an RV park or campground, you have to consider a range of federal and local restrictions. For specific local restrictions, you should contact your local government agency to ask what specific permits or regulations are required before you start the planning process for your facility.

You may need to meet specific zoning requirements that will factor into the planning process for your facility. In addition, there are general legal considerations when it comes to things like sanitation issues and ADA requirements. Let's consider some of the general legal requirements that are required, no matter where you plan to start your facility. While RVs are self-contained, an RV facility is still required to provide all the support services. This means roadways, utilities, bathrooms, garbage facilities, and sewage dump stations.

Code Requirements

New facility designs are influenced by many codes that you need to consider. Health Department codes address public health concerns, zoning codes address permitted use of the land, development codes address the construction of the facility including access and stormwater management, building codes regular structures and ADA access, and utility codes regular utility requirements. Let's look at all of these in a little more detail to help you see what goes into designing, planning, and building your RV park or campground.

Health Department Codes

These codes regulate public environmental health issues. There are five main code requirements that you need to be aware of when planning an RV facility.

First, there needs to be proper grading of stormwater away from sites so that there is no standing water in or runoff through sites.

Then there are Campground Density Limits, which is defined as the maximum number of sites allowed per acre of land. The total number of sites allowed is calculated by multiplying the permitted density by the amount of land available for development. In some jurisdictions, you can only use "usable" land for these calculations.

Third are potable water requirements that impact services, connections, and availability. The regulations determine which sites are given potable water connections, what protection these connections have, backflow prevention devices, and requirements for potable water stations.

Regulations also set non-potable water requirements for signage and separation from potable water sources. Non-potable water is allowed for vehicle washing or rinsing at sewage dump stations.

Lastly, there are codes regarding sewage disposal requirements and the protection of sewer service connections. Even if every site has a sewage connection, there may still be a requirement for a sewage dump station, this will depend on local requirements. A sewage dump station may take up the space of one or two sites, so you should definitely know this before designing your facility.

Required Services

All RV facilities are required to provide basic services such as bathing, garbage collection, sewage disposal sites, and fire protection. All these need to be put in place according to state/local codes and regulations.

Bathhouses

Bathing regulations are met by providing showers, sinks, and toilets. The number of sites your facility has will determine the number of showers, sinks, and toilets you need to install. The layout of your facility will also impact the number of bathhouses and their locations. How many sites are within the service area will determine the exact number of each shower, sink, and toilet in a bathhouse.

Your local regulatory agency will be responsible for defining the bathhouse service area, but it is often the number of sites within a 250-foot radius of the bathhouse. This is measured in one of two ways:

1. The radius is measured from the center of the building, the nearest entrance, or the nearest corner of the building according to local ordinances.

2. The distance of the route a guest must take to get to the bathhouse.

Obviously, the method of calculation will have a big impact on the size of each bathhouse and where they are located within your facility. Another way to think of this is the fact that the closer your sites are to each other, the more showers, sinks, and toilets you'll need in the nearby bathhouses. For example, a long and narrow property with bathroom access limited to two to three sides will require more bathhouses that are smaller in size than a property that has sites surrounding a larger bathhouse.

Sewage Dump Stations

These are required at all RV parks and campgrounds. Typically, they are located at dedicated pull-through sites. High volume campgrounds may need a dump station located between two service drives in order to service two RVs at a time. Sewage dump stations often need a trapped four-inch sewer riser pipe connected to an approved sewage system. It is often installed in a concrete apron that is sloped to provide drainage and has a hinged cover. It is also required to have a water supply outlet for wash down. The washdown hose should also have an immediately adjacent posted sign "WATER NOT SAFE FOR DRINKING."

Garbage Collection

This is regulated differently based on local codes. It can vary from garbage cans to large screened-in dumpsters. In some local areas, recycling bins are also a requirement. However, all facilities are required to have some form of garbage collection.

Garbage Cans

Some local ordinances require a garbage can at each site. If this is the case in your area, then animal-proof cans that are secured are your best bet. This can be a can chained to a post with a locking lid or a can inside a metal or wooden cage. There are plenty of designs available, but you want to choose one that is easily accessible by guests and easy to maintain by yourself or your staff.

Dumpsters

This option provides a larger storage capacity and fewer pick-up locations. However, the trade-off is that they will require a larger area in order to be accessible by a garbage truck. These will also need to be strategically placed within your facility since most guests won't want to stay at the site next to a dumpster. In some areas, the dumpsters may be required to be screened from view by walls or fences. Some local areas may take it a step further by requiring the screening to be matched to the architectural style of the buildings in the facility. Local codes will give you the design requirements.

Recycling Bins

In most jurisdictions, recycling bins are now required as well. Often these must be co-located with the garbage collection bins. Again, you can look at local codes for all the specific requirements.

Utilities

Electrical is provided in a weatherproof box and supplied in a 20-, 30- and 50-amp circuit. If there is no 50-amp service available, then the RVer will need to use an adapter to connect to the 30-amp service, and this will restrict the usage of some equipment such as air conditioners and heaters.

Water service is provided through one or two hose bibs on a half-inch water pipe.

Sewer service is provided through a four-inch sewer service connection. Most RVs have a three-inch hose with a four-inch adapter connector.

Electrical and water lines need to be buried 36 inches below the surface in order to be protected from anything being driven into the ground.

Facility Access

Depending on the roadway where your facility is located, the access from the public roads will be regulated by the county, Parrish, or State. Depending on the size of your facility, one or more turn lanes may be required. Other things that may be regulated include the speed on the main road, the roadway gradient, number of lanes, peak hour traffic counts, and site distances. Since most RVs don't decelerate quickly or turn quickly, most entrances need right and left turn lanes for safety.

Most RV facilities have only one entrance because it allows management and staff to monitor and control access. However, some regulations will require two or more access points for emergency purposes in the event that the main entrance is obstructed. Your local codes will determine access requirements. Sometimes local ordinances will allow for a divided 4-lane entrance since two exit lanes can be used for ingress/egress during an emergency if needed.

ADA Issues

Along with the increase in RVers, there is also an increase in physically challenged RVers. This requires ADA compliance in areas such as specially designed sites, accessible bathhouses, and ADA ramps. While these are the same issues that are faced by any other commercial development, the challenge here is providing them while also providing your guests with an enjoyable outdoor experience. Often engineers place ADA sites next to the bathhouses. While this is an efficient design, it can detract from the outdoor experience of your disabled guests.

This puts them close to the noise and increased traffic. This is where your design and landscaping skills will come into play. ADA sites should be no closer to the bathhouses than to provide ease of ADA access, but still be far enough away to provide a pleasant outdoor experience. Placing a sidewalk through heavy vegetation with signage that notifies guests it goes to an ADA site can be one option.

Pedestrian Clear Zones

If possible, it can be good to provide a striped pedestrian lane alongside the pavement for pedestrians to use. Interior pedestrian routes should be well maintained so they can be easily traveled by people of all ages. Vegetation should be maintained to avoid hiding places for both animals and people. Low-level lighting is best to illuminate the path without providing a disturbing level of light to nearby sites.

Host Campsites

If you plan to use host campsites, they will need to be strategically placed and used to provide security and assistance by employees or volunteers. The host campsites should be in a place to provide good visibility to as many sites as possible. They should also have clear signage to indicate that they are a host site and available to provide assistance. These sites can be a great way to provide protection from vandalism, noise, and other minor annoyances.

In addition to making sure you meet all the legal and utility requirements, you also need to give thought to what amenities you will provide. This is about more than simply choosing what to provide for your guests, and often amenities can influence the revenue of your facility and whether or not guests will choose you over other nearby accommodations.

Amenity Considerations

This is an area where you benefit from doing your research first and determining who your target audience is going to be at your facility. If you are looking to attract families, then you need to have a set of attractions that will appeal to these individuals, such as a playground, game room, and/or a swimming pool. However, these may not be the same amenity choices you would make if your focus was on adults without children. While you might still have a pool, you may consider adding a spa as well.

If your focus is more on the retirement crowd, you may want to consider a putting green or an indoor room with a pool. Perhaps you might install a library or a computer room.

Also, you want to keep in mind the natural location of your park when deciding what amenities to offer. For example, if you are close to a lake, then you may want to offer boating options. Remember that amenities are often one of the biggest influences in why people choose an RV park over other accommodations.

Should You Have a Clubhouse?

Most people who travel by RV are social. Often they are a part of groups with similar interests. This is an important thing to keep in mind when thinking about amenities at your facility. Having the facilities at your park to support the basic needs of a decent-sized group will help you to attract these types of individuals. The main part of this is to have a clubhouse. Often this will include basic kitchen facilities and a place to host group meetings or other similar events. The more attractive and extensive your clubhouse facilities, the more success it will have at attracting RV clubs for events at your facility. This can increase your occupancy during peak seasons and also give you a chance to attract people during the slow seasons as well.

At the same time, it is a good idea to consider those who aren't a part of the RV lifestyle yet. Just because the focus of your facility is the RV traveler, doesn't mean you can't make extra revenue by attracting other travelers as well. Consider adding other accommodations to help attract people that want to try out the RV lifestyle for a few nights.

Renting Out RVs and Cabins

While most of your occupancy is going to be RV travelers, you may want to consider adding cabin and/or RV rentals to attract even more guests. This may seem the opposite of the business you are trying to start, but often RV parks see an increase in visitors when they offer more accommodation choices. Let's look at some of the pros and cons of offering cabin and/or RV rentals to generate additional occupancy and revenue at your RV park or campground.

The Pros

In today's modern world, people are accustomed to a few things. When people choose to go camping or enjoy the outdoors, they are often faced with having to go without internet, which for most, is a major issue. However, if you take away a hot shower and a climate-controlled building, a lot of people choose to forgo the vacation experience. For these individuals, offering a rental cabin may be the only way to get them to make a reservation with your facility.

In addition, as the retirement generation gets older, it gets harder and harder to stay outdoors. Even an RV may require a lot of work to set up and hookup for those who are aging.

When you offer cabins, you will allow people to enjoy the outdoors without having to put a lot of stress on them. Even if people are still willing to live and stay in an RV, having cabins means that family members who don't enjoy the RV lifestyle can still come and stay with them. In addition, having different accommodations can increase your reservations in the offseason.

The Cons

Renting RVs and cabins can be difficult from a maintenance point of view. You are likely going to be renting RV units to people who want to experience the lifestyle but have never been in an RV before. If something goes wrong with an RV or cabin, you need to fix it fast. If you don't have the ability to make fast repairs, then you'll have to cancel reservations on short notice, and this can have a negative impact on your business.

Also, RVs and cabins will require you to hire a cleaning crew; unless you are comfortable doing this yourself. This can be challenging if you have a fast turnover of guests in these accommodations.

Lastly, in certain states, you will need to pay for a hotel certification when you rent RVs and/or cabins. This means you'll have to pay an additional tax for units that you rent, and you'll have a lot more paperwork to do at the end of the year.

In the end, it is a decision of what works for you. If it seems like you can deal with the cons, then the revenue of renting RVs and/or cabins can be a good investment for your business. Otherwise, it may be too costly of an investment for your business, and you should look for other revenue streams to supplement your business. Let's look at a few of these other options.

Additional RV Park Features to Offer

With nearly a million households going on an RV trip each year, you can attract a good chunk of these travelers by offering a few unique amenities that help you to stand out from the competition. When you own an RV park or campground, there are a lot of money-making opportunities you can implement than you might realize. While your strongest asset will remain the renting of sites, you should consider adding in some auxiliary products and services to help increase your revenue. For your guests, you'll seem like a one-stop-shop for their outdoor or RV experience and will enjoy seeing these additional products and services. Let's look at some ideas to help you get started.

Simply setting aside an area in your park for a stage or theater can open up a range of possibilities and can be a versatile option. There are a number of activities that can be added here. You can invite bands/singers for a concert night. You can offer plays or hold special holiday talent shows. Outdoor stages and theaters are a big attraction at a lot of RV parks or campgrounds.

Consider adding additional water features. Even if you are near a lake or other body of water, there are still some pleasing water features you can add to attract guests. This can include things like splash pads, water slides, and game areas. These will increase your chance of visitors in the summer months. Plus, it gives people an alternative if they don't want to go into the lake.

Sports are a popular outdoor activity for those who live the RV lifestyle. Especially if you are trying to attract the active outdoor focused traveler. Even within the retirement community, there are certain outdoor sports that might be of interest. Consider adding areas such as a basketball court, horseshoes, volleyball, mini-golf, shuffleboard, or any other number of sports activities. Most of the time, providing your guests with an outdoor activity doesn't cost you much in terms of time and money.

Similar to sports, consider putting in an obstacle course. This can be good for both kids and adults, plus it can be the stepping stone to offering to host summer camps. You could also rent out your obstacle course for fitness groups for training or events.

Lastly, consider adding a general store or restaurant. People often forget things when packing for a trip or after a day of traveling; they are tired and don't want to take the time to prepare a meal. When you have this one-stop-shop experience, your guests won't have to go hunting around the local area that is unfamiliar to them for something they can easily get within your facility. Consider popular snack food options that you can offer to help increase your revenue.

Top Snacks to Offer

When you spend time outdoors, you get hungry, and there is nothing better than enjoying delicious snacks while spending time in the beautiful outdoors. Cooking when you're outdoors isn't the easiest, even if you are in an RV. Offering the following foods can help you offer a convenient and tasty treat for your guests and increase revenue for your facility.

S'mores Kits

S'mores are always a must whenever you are enjoying a camping adventure either in a tent or in an RV. However, most people will forget some part of the ingredients needed for this experience. Have everything a guest needs to make this tasty treat: marshmallows, chocolate, graham crackers, grill skewers, lighters, and even firewood. You can even choose to bundle these items.

Popsicles

On a hot day, nothing is more enjoyable than a popsicle. No matter what age, people will want to enjoy these. Have a supply on hand during the warmer months, and you're sure to get some additional sales.

Burgers

Most people think of grilling burgers on an outdoor fire pit. Again, this is a dish where people may forget one or more ingredients. Have buns, burger meat, cheese, and a range of fixings available so your guests will have everything they need. If possible, consider getting your supplies from local sources since this is popular with the millennial generation.

Hot Dogs

Another popular memory for the traveler is cooking hot dogs over an open fire. Again, have a range of condiments available along with the hot dogs and buns. Maybe even have some sticks ready for roasting over the fire. Your guests will be happy that you have everything they need.

Trail Mix

Most people who travel by RV also enjoy outdoor activities like hiking and kayaking. For these guests, you want to have a few options for on-the-go snacks that they can easily grab before activities. Consider individual-sized packets of things like trail mix in a range of flavors so that you can offer something for every preference.

Potatoes

There are plenty of dishes that can be made with potato and it is a staple of a lot of side dishes. Potatoes are also a cheap food option. Consider selling potatoes and other things like foil and prongs so people can cook them how they choose to on the open fire pit.

Beans

Eating beans while sitting around an open fire is another great outdoor experience. Beans are also easy to make, no matter what your level of experience with an RV kitchen or outdoor cooking. They are also tasty and filling, the perfect camping food.

Queso

Another thing people will enjoy is snack food, especially if they are having a get-together. Offer things like tortilla chips, Velveeta, and canned tomatoes. Provide everything people need to make simple and tasty nachos. You may also want to offer pots and/or kitchen supply rentals in case people forget these.

Candy

Everyone enjoys a sweet treat at some point. If family or friends are visiting, it is also a great gift option. Offer a range of selections for people to choose from. You can also look into the option of getting candy or chocolate branded with your logo on it. This will be a popular selling point for your guests.

Peanut Butter

Whether making sandwiches or just having as a spoonful snack, peanut butter is a great option. It is simple and filling. Have this staple on hand. Be sure to include a few other nut spreads and alternatives in case of people with allergies

No matter what food you choose to sell at your store, just remember you want to try and anticipate as much as possible what your guests may need. When you do this, you are offering your guests a memorable and carefree experience. This will lead to a favorable experience and potentially return guests or referrals for other guests.

Once you have a good handle on what your park design is going to be and have an idea of the basics you need to have installed, there are a few other things to consider. You'll want to determine what to charge for a site, what your operating cost is going to be, and who your target audience is going to be. There is a lot of little things to consider as you plan out the start of your RV facility. Let's consider these areas next.

What to Consider in Planning Your Facility

When you are planning out your RV facility, the thing you want to do is consider what RVers are "looking for" when choosing an RV park or campground. While there isn't a single right answer or one that would reflect the preference of everyone who travels by RV, there are some things that can help increase your chances of being the go-to destination for RVers. Let's look at some of the basics, so you know what to consider when designing and setting up your facility.

An Inviting Environment

Perhaps one of the most powerful things when it comes to choosing a facility for RVers is the first impression. This is for the RVers who are looking for a place while traveling, do they turn into a place or keep going down the road? It can be difficult to list all the possible factors involved in a first impression. Rather, it is easier to consider what would make travelers pass up your facility for the next one down the road. Obvious signs of construction, overcrowded streets or sites, a facility that doesn't feel "secure," buildings that appear to need repair or broken vehicles. These are some things that would certainly make people immediately head to another facility. So make sure you do what you can to make a good first impression to the RV traveler looking for a space to spend the night.

Site Spacing

You likely have already addressed this in your design and planning phase, but if you haven't, then now is the time to consider it. For economic reasons, you'll likely need to design your sites for greater density. However, you need to find the tradeoff between a high-density facility and an individual site with privacy. You don't want to give off the appearance of being nothing more than a parking lot for RVs. Site layout is definitely challenging, but with proper landscaping, the site spacing can be closer without actually feeling or appearing like it is. In addition, diagonal or off-set sites can avoid the feeling of being lined up in a parking lot. It is also a good idea to always have a few pull-through sites for those who aren't comfortable backing up in an RV.

Friendly Staff

Since there is no "perfect" RV facility that is going to meet all the right preferences for every traveler. The sense and reception that people get when they first enter the office can make all the difference. Ensure you hire staff that greets all the guests as a friend. This will quickly help your guests get over any preferences that are missing. Most people who travel by RV are looking to meet new people and are often very friendly. This means they will respond in a positive way to staff who are obviously "people persons." While checking people in, strike up a conversation, and help the guests to feel at home.

The RV Site

Nothing brings more dread in an RV traveler than being assigned a site in a park they've never been to before. When pulling into a site, a guest is going to quickly notice how well laid out a facility really is. This is another area that may have already been addressed in the planning phase, but if not needs to be considered now. Are the hookups in the right spot? Are the sites level? Do they appear welcoming? All of this is essential to a good first impression on the RV traveler. No one wants to arrive, only to have to go through a difficult and extensive setup process. Make your site as inviting in appearance and as easy for hookup as possible so your guests will have a convenient and memorable experience.

Settling In

After your guests have settled in, they will soon want to get out and explore the surrounding area. What there is to do will depend on the individual guest and what they prefer to do. Consider offering your guests brochures and maps of local activities at check-in or having these available in the office. Also, having a friendly and knowledgeable staff who can guide guests is helpful. Plus, giving your guests a number of things to see and do in the surrounding area may inspire them to stay a few extra nights, especially if you've met all of the above requirements to have a great RV facility that travelers will enjoy.

Pricing, Reservations, and Policies

Another important thing to consider in today's modern society is how your reservations are made. While RVers will certainly pick a facility simply by driving by while on a trip, there are those who are researching and planning a trip in advance through the internet. For this reason, it can be a good idea to offer online reservations for your facility.

Online Reservations

Everyone goes online these days for a variety of reasons. One of these is to make vacation reservations or plan a vacation. This should be enough reason to start an online reservation system for your RV facility. But in case you need a few more reasons, consider the following facts.

In 2016, the number of travel bookings made online in the United States was over 148 million. With an online reservation system, your RV facility can take advantage of these increasing numbers.

In 2016, 40% of those who booked online did so 1-5 days in advance of their stay and 24% booked on the day of their stay. If you have a website, consider offering a coupon that offers a discount for booking at that time; chances are good people will book with your facility. Most people are looking to make reservations the day they are searching, and they often don't want to call around. People want convenience. You can give them this through an online reservation system and make money for your facility.

A poll showed that 30% of millennial travelers were worried that costs would increase if they took too long to book a trip, and only 19% or less of people booked travel plans within a week or less of their departure date. This means that if you want, you can offer the same rate for those who book in advance and charge more for those who wait to book.

The largest percentage, 78%, of people booking in advance were those who traveled during the holidays such as Thanksgiving, Memorial Day, and the Fourth of July. If you have an online reservation system and a good website showcasing what you have to offer, then you are sure to get plenty of reservations during these holidays.

Even if you aren't online, there is a good chance that your facility is on Yelp, Facebook, or Trip Advisor. It is crucial that you have a website for your facility. Linking directly to these sites will increase your chance of online reservations. We'll discuss more about this when it comes to marketing and advertising for your park.

Today, having an online reservation system for your facility is a must. The process is fairly easy and can be done yourself or through a paid professional. Guests want everything to be convenient, and you can offer this by making the booking process quick and easy. When their visit with you starts out convenient before they even get to your park, then this is going to increase their memorable experience at your facility. However, what do you plan to charge for your sites? How can you determine costs? How do you handle deposits? Let's consider these next.

Determining the Cost for a Site

The average rate for an RV site is about $20, with additional costs for more than two people. Most parks offer a weekly rate that typically offers the seventh day for free and a monthly rate that often varies depending on the park. Having a pricing policy in place is important so that you and your employees can easily quote a rate to someone who calls for the information. The best way to determine this pricing policy and find out what you should charge per site is determined by using yield management. It will also help you to maximize profits.

The thing to keep in mind is that when using yield management, you may lose a few customers. However, you won't be able to set up a pricing policy that pleases everyone. For example, if you have 100 sites and you charge $2 more per day for a one day holiday, you will increase your income by $200. If people felt the cost was too expensive for a holiday weekend, you may end up with say eight empty sites that you aren't able to fill with new customers, but you would still be ahead. The reality is that as long as you can provide value for the price charged, then people won't avoid your facility. Consider how many times you hear complaints about your rates and then adjust accordingly.

While it is a simple matter to raise your rates, the hard part is telling your customers what the rate is if you have many variables. There are a few ways you can do this. One is to give a range and be upfront when telling them that the rate isn't higher on the weekend, but rather they are getting a discount during the week. For example, the July 4th weekend isn't costing more; rather, it is now the regular rate, and customers can still get a discount if they stay on a different weekend. Another option is to offer a standard site for a cheaper rate to those who complain about the rates.

Keeping Track of Your Rates

When using a manual system for reservations and registration, it can be difficult to track your rates. For this reason, I strongly recommend that you have only a few different price points to keep things straight. This can be assessing a surcharge for major holidays and setting only two types of sites. However, if you are using a computerized system, which I also highly recommend, then you can experiment with as many price points as you want.

When you have a computerized system, you can use a yield management pricing policy. This will add about 25%

more to your bottom line. But how does this system work? There is a lot of research needed in order to determine the different price points you can use and how you want to have them set up. If you used the same manner that hotels use, then you would have about a hundred different prices for people staying at your facility in a year. Realistically, you don't need or want this many price points, about half will do. If you aren't comfortable doing all this math on your own, then you can hire a consultant to help.

In order to manage all these price points, it is best to have a computerized reservation and registration system. If you use a manual system, it will still be doable, but it will be difficult to manage. However, even once you figure out the cost for each site, there still remains the bigger issue of how to handle the deposit process.

Setting Up Deposit Rules

One thing that I heard come up a lot when I was starting an RV facility is the debate over the deposit policy. There is no real right or wrong answer when it comes to what your reservation deposit policy should be. If your sites aren't rented and/or when a guest is a no-show, you will lose both money and time. A reservation deposit is one way to deter guests from not showing up, but it can also cause some guests to hold back on reserving a site. Finding the right balance can be difficult. There are three main deposit policies that most RV parks use. Let's look at these three and discuss the pros and cons of each so you can determine what the right policy is for your facility.

One-Night Stays

Even during a single night stay, guests should pay something at the time of reservation. While staying at an RV facility is a fairly cheap option for vacations, you don't want your guests to spend all their money right away. However, you want to ensure your guests commit to showing up for their stay. For these, it can be a good idea to mandate a small fixed amount during the reservation. This is typically a charge of about thirty to forty dollars.

Pros

This will give you some money upfront for the reservation and tells you the guests are committed. It also ensures your guests won't have to break the bank just to make a reservation. This seems to be a good policy.

Cons

This may be a confusing policy for future guests, but is often a small enough amount that guests won't mind. This means that some people will be fine with not showing up and losing their deposit. While you will get to keep the deposit, you have also lost the time it will take to remarket the site to another potential guest. When a guest doesn't show up, you only have a day to find another guest to take the site. If not, then you'll lose out on the revenue from the site.

Payment Plan

When you use a payment plan, you need to set a schedule for guests to make payments for their reservation stay. This is similar to a layaway plan. The guest will book a site online for a long-term stay. They will need to make an initial deposit for a fixed amount at the time of making the reservation. At this point, no one else can book the site for the same days. Then you set a percent of the reservation charges that need to be paid by a certain date before their check-in date. At that point, they either have to pay the remaining balance two weeks before their arrival, or the balance is due upon their arrival.

Pros

This option can attract guests to book longer stays, especially if you have in-demand amenities, activities, and local attractions to keep people entertained for a longer stay. A group of four can take up a site for a month, and the cost could easily be a thousand dollars or more. Plus, a longer stay offers a greater chance to upsell on things like services, equipment rentals, or unique activities. Paying for an entire reservation fee of a thousand or more upfront can be difficult for some people. With a payment plan, they won't have to pay as much upon making the reservation and can have the entire cost paid off a few weeks before their trip, which means they are more likely to book a stay.

Cons

Having a complex payment plan can make your reservation operations and even your bookkeeping a little more tricky. You'll have to keep track of payment schedules for all reservations that use it. Imagine having to send a bill to each long term guest for their monthly stay, each based on their arrival dates. Updating your payment schedule will become a daily task. Plus, you have the added hassle of getting ahold for the client and getting payment information. Based on all the work involved, you may rethink implementing this deposit policy.

100% Reservation Fee Upfront

This is a popular option within the tourism and lodging industry for years. There is no secret behind this method. The guest simply pays for 100% of their reservation charge upfront and in full at the time of booking. This is the same whether they book by phone or through your online booking site. This means you get all the money upon making the reservation.

Pros

There are plenty of good things about this deposit policy and is the one I strongly recommend. First, guests are already used to this policy within the industry if they have stayed at a hotel or other type of lodging before. The other plus is that you get all of your money upfront. You can then use the money to make improvements, cover payroll, or other needed costs. It gives you guest added incentive to show up for their reservation.

Keep in mind that you are basically offering a product that expires since each night a site goes unreserved is a night you won't be able to sell. This is why you should combine this deposit policy with a cancellation and refund policy that allows you to reserve the spot to another guest if the original guest cancels. This is a win-win situation for you as a business. You will get all the money for the site, plus you'll be able to rent it to someone else. Even if you need to refund a cancellation, you will have time to resell the site to another guest.

Cons

It's obvious that you will need to deliver on the promise to have a site available for the guests under this deposit system. If you have a manual reservation system, it is possible to have human error or smudged ink lead to issues with the sites getting double booked. This can be a bad position for you as a business and can damage your reputation. However, if you use a computerized system, then the chances of errors are less.

Consider the pros and cons of each of these deposit policies carefully to determine which is best for you. Once you implement a deposit system and set up a payment policy, you can move on to considering your ongoing operating costs. Once you consider these costs, you may need to go back and adjust your payment policy.

The last thing you need to consider before opening your RV park is to set up a Rules of Conduct for your guests. This can be an important step that shouldn't be overlooked when starting an RV park or campground.

Rules of Conduct

Before your guests start arriving, it is a great idea to have some established RV park rules. The rules need to be reasonable and clearly stated in a way that is effective and still "guest friendly." It is possible to have all three of these objectives met when creating RV park rules. Establishing rules ensures your guests will have a pleasant experience, but also provides your park with a positive statement. Let's consider what you need to establish the rules of conduct for your park.

Often park rules are established with little thought about the image they will portray of the park. Keep in mind that the rules will paint a picture of both you and your park. Most RVers will be glad to abide by a reasonable set of rules that lay out acceptable standards of how one should behave. This can include how pets are supervised, speed limits within the park, parking, noise, and other matters. It is also important that whatever rules you create, you are actually able to enforce.

You need to go a step beyond just creating reasonable rules. You also need to "present" them in the best possible way. Present the rules in a clear way that show the park owner is ensuring the enjoyment and comfort of all guests. Don't simply list the rules of no's; rather, make them sound reasonable. Motivated RVers will be more likely to conform to rules and standards when they are pleasantly worded. You'll also be able to avoid unintended subliminal messages when showing clearly that the rules reflect the bad behavior of others who have stayed at the park.

Ongoing Operating Costs

A vital part of successfully running an RV park or campground is in understanding the ongoing cost involved in operating the business. This allows you to set your pricing so you can maintain the costs needed to run the facility while also having a buffer in case of unplanned expenses.

There are a number of factors that go into running an RV park or campground that can determine the ongoing expenses. While most facilities are typically inexpensive to operate, there are others that can be quite pricey. Some of these factors include location, zoning, nearby competition, level of amenities, number of average guests, impacts of the seasons, and the availability of necessary resources. In general, some common expenses you should be prepared for include the following:

- Mortgage or lease payments for the land.

- Taxes on land, buildings, income, and sales.

- Utilities including water, sewer, electric, cable, and internet.

- Maintenance on the land, buildings, utilities, frontage, and signage.

- The cost of maintaining and training employees.

- Marketing and advertising costs, including local, national, print, digital, website, and social media.

- The cost of dealing with city and county regulations.

- The cost of maintaining legal counsel or dealing with any potential legal issues from customers.

- Property, liability, and disaster insurance.

- The cost of equipment maintenance.

- Operating costs of equipment and sites.

Most public agencies that run RV parks need to raise costs in order to cover expenses. However, as a private business, you have an advantage in this area. You have the option of making drastic changes to your cost structure in order to increase your revenue without having to increase your rates. Before you make any changes, you need to analyze previous expenses or, in the case of starting a new park, the projected expenses. Categorize these costs and then set a budget. If this seems like it's too difficult of a task, then you can hire or work with a CPA or tax professional to help you with this financial analysis.

Operating any kind of business has costs associated with it, and it is important that you know and understand these costs. Knowing the costs is important to maintaining a viable business. Even if you have an understanding of your ongoing costs, make sure you have a way to plan and prepare for unexpected costs as well. In addition to costs, you also want to consider and define the operating hours for your business.

Determining Operating Hours

When it comes to operating hours for your business, there are two main areas to consider. First, you need to consider your general operating hours and whether or not you should set up a curfew for your guests. Second, you need to consider the effects of seasonality of your business and how to prepare for the slower winter months. Let's look at these two areas in a little more detail.

Setting Up a Curfew

When it comes to curfews, finding the right balance for your facility can be a bit tricky. You need to find a balance between resident and guest schedules, especially when some guests are there for leisure, and others are there on a more long-term basis. In addition, there are plenty of criteria to consider when setting curfew rules such as lights out, quiet times, work hours, and even check-in and out times. Consider the following when setting up your own curfew rules:

Keep in mind that a lot of noise occurs during check-in and check out, especially if there are RVs close to the new guests. Consider offering a complimentary breakfast to early arrivals and ask them to wait until quiet time is over to respect the guests that are already there. This can be really important on the weekends when people are more likely to sleep later.

In addition to guests, make sure you consider your own work around the campground. This can be more challenging if you are relying on workers outside your facility. No matter what the work is, you should follow your own work curfew. Anything before 8 am on weekdays and 10 am on weekends is considered early for most. Therefore, wait on most of the loud work until everyone should be awake.

Keeping fires lit and lights on can be a problem for other facility guests. A general rule that most parks have is 11 pm for lights out and 12 am for fires. You may be able to let this rule slide for a little bit, but drinking around a campfire can cause louder activities later into the evening.

If you think guests may not respond well to "curfew" rules, then you might want to consider adjusting your facility to have an area for those who will be up later or sleep in later. Then when guests arrive, you can ask what their schedule will be like and place them accordingly.

In the end, you want to base your curfew rules on the guests. Consider the target audience for your park and who the majority of your guests will be when setting up your curfew rules. You'll always have some who don't fit these rules, but having them in place for the majority of your guests will make it more enjoyable for them.

Dealing with the Seasons

One of the biggest concerns you need to address when owning an RV facility is the length of the "season." For example, the snowbird parks in Arizona are packed full in February and then become a ghost town in August. In the northern areas, most RV facilities have a brisk summer season and then either close or operate with very few guests in the winter months. There are few facilities that aren't affected by the seasons, such as those in California and Florida.

If your park is located anywhere else in the United States, you'll experience a high demand "in season" and low occupancy in the "low season." You need to know how long the high season will be; you can get a realistic assessment of this factor by using reliable financial projections.

All parks will have to deal with some form of a "low season," and it is important to have a strategy in place for lowering the impact of this time. If you have good group facilities, then you can offer promotional events to RV groups to attract them during the off season. You can also offer seasonal promotional pricing to at least help pay the utility bills during the off season. You can allow "seasonal" guests to stay for favorable rates at extended periods during the off season, but this can come with some risks as you'll often be opening yourself to individuals looking more for a housing situation rather than an RV vacation. No matter what you choose to do to make money in the off season, there are some things you need to do in order to prepare your facility for the winter months.

Find Potential Money Makers

Just because the weather isn't as favorable in the winter months doesn't mean people can't still enjoy the outdoors. So look for ways to increase revenue at your park based on how your guests can enjoy the outdoors. For example, if you have fire pits, you can sell more things like s'mores supplies. If your area has a slope for sledding, you can sell sleds. Even the most prepared campers may find the nights colder than expected, so you can have clothing items to keep them warm like socks, gloves, and hats.

Water

If you rent out cabins, then you need to properly shut them down for the winter months or prepare them to stay open. The number one priority is to ensure your water pipes don't crack. The best option is to drain your pipes and then blow out the remaining water with the compressor. In addition to the main water pipes, don't forget about winterizing water heaters and garden hoses as well. If you can't flush out your pipes and shut down your cabins, then make sure your pipes are well insulated. Even if you feel comfortable doing this yourself, you should pay a plumber to do it for you. In the end, it will save you a lot of time and money.

Heating

If you are going to keep cabins open for the winter, then it can be a good idea to keep the heat running. Having the heat at about 55 to 60 degrees in the winter months will prevent the pipes from freezing and will also prevent the grout in tiles in the bathrooms and kitchens from buckling. While this may cost your more in utilities during the off season, it will be far cheaper than replacing the plumbing or tile.

Storage

Walk your grounds and speak with your guests, make sure anything that isn't needed is properly stored for the winter. For example, if you have multiple community grills, then you can maybe store all but one for use by guests. If boats or kayaks aren't needed, then store them with one a few left for easy access.

Repairs

All small repairs should be done before winter, so you don't spend a good portion of your springtime preparing for the busy summer months.

In addition to thinking about the seasonality of your park and the pricing, a very important thing to consider is who your target audience is going to be.

Defining and knowing what type of guests you're going to plan to attract will help with a lot of planning, design, and overall considerations.

Identifying and Obtaining Customers

There are two things that lead to the success of an RV park: it is either located near high volumes of RV traffic, or it is close to a popular destination area. Where your RV park is located will determine which of these two areas you need to use to succeed. From here, you can determine your target audience and focus your efforts on getting the volume of guests you need to be successful. Let's look at these two types of facilities.

The first is the facility that is located near a high volume of RV traffic. These are often considered the "overnight" RV parks. You will have a steady flow of RVs passing by en route to another location. These guests aren't interested in long term stays, but rather just want to rest for a day and plan to get back on the road the following morning. The best "overnight" locations should focus on making a stay so pleasant and inviting with a focus on the special features of the surrounding area. This can help persuade some RV guests to stay a few more nights in order to see the sites. You might also get a few who will stop by again on their return trip.

The second is the "destination" RV park. These facilities typically don't have a high volume of RV traffic within a short distance. Rather, these types of facilities rely on the special attraction offered by the area. This is the plan RVers go to set up base camp for days, weeks, or more while they explore all the local area has to offer. A good example of a "destination" park are the snowbird parks in the southwest as well as the coastal parks. RVers will typically spend up to several months in one location.

What if the location of your facility doesn't meet either of these descriptions? All hope is not lost, but it will be more of a challenge. You will likely need to put a little more into your marketing efforts in order to attract RVers to the area, but it can be done. The goal is to analyze your target audience: is it the overnight traveler or the destination? Perhaps it has a little of both. When you know your target audience's type and motivation, then you can implement this into a variety of planning and design phases for your facility.

Now that you have the basics needed for your RV facility, you should start looking at the business essentials. There is a lot that goes into starting your own business. Let's consider all the necessary things you need in order to start a new business.

Business Essentials

When it comes to starting a business, there is a lot that needs to go into it. You need to have a well-written business plan to assist through the startup process and to grow. You also need to fill out proper registration, get the right permits and licenses, open a business bank account, and have the proper level of insurance. Let's look at all of the essentials you need and how to get them started.

Business Name and Logo

The name and logo you choose when starting your business are two of the most important decisions you'll make. They are nearly as important as what you are trying to sell. A well-chosen name and logo will stay in the minds of your customers and remind them of what you have to offer. The best name and logo will allow you to stand out from the competition and make people think of you first when they are looking for an RV park. Let's first look at how you can choose a great RV facility name.

Take a few moments to brainstorm business name ideas and write down everything that comes to you. Even if the name doesn't seem to fit, you may need it to help narrow your list later, or you may use part of it.

It is a good idea to choose a short name. Business names are best if they are short enough to be easy to remember and write. Not only will this make it easier for your customers to remember you, but it can also make it easier when choosing a website domain.

In addition, the name you choose should be easy to spell. Customers can have a hard time finding a business on the internet or in directories if it has a complicated spelling.

You also want to try for a memorable name, one that will help your customers remember you and have you stand out from the competition. A name that is hard to remember means your customers may go to the competition simply because they can't remember what your business was called.

Your business name should match your business image. For example, an RV park will likely want a name that inspires images or feelings of the great outdoors.

Similarly, you want to choose a name that makes it obvious what your business is for so potential guests won't have to guess what your park is like. For example, if you are offering a luxury RV park, this should be reflected in the name, so people don't assume they are only staying at an RV campground.

Once you have a name in mind, you need to make sure the business name isn't already in use. Contact your state's business registration or a fictitious name agency in order to see if your potential business name is already in use. You should also check to see if the name is trademarked, which means you'll have to choose another name. You can check for trademarks through a Patent and Trademark Depository Library or online.

After ensuring no one else is using your business name, take the time to speak it out loud. This will help you to determine if you like the way it sounds. Take the time to write it out and think about it. Once you are sure it is right for your business, then you can settle on it and focus on creating a business logo.

Start by taking the time to examine the logos of your competition. You want to do this to both make sure you don't choose something similar and to help your logo stand out for customers.

Next, decide what image you want to convey with the logo. Remember that your logo will imprint a specific image in the minds of your guests. This is why you should consider your customers' perception of color and match colors to the image you want to convey.

The third step is to create a few different logos or ask someone to design a few for you. This allows you to compare several options and find one that best represents your facility. Ask your family and friends what they think. You may find that what looks great to you, actually has a negative image for other people. It is always good to have a few additional opinions.

It is also important that you have the logo blown up and shrunk down in size. This will help you to see how your logo appears on different marketing materials. You may think a logo looks great, but when shrunk down for marketing materials, it is no longer clear. You should also consider your logo in both color and black and white since you never know what materials you may be printing your logo on, and you want to make sure you are completely happy with your logo choice before committing to it.

After you have a strong business name and logo, the next essentials you want to focus on are your vision and mission statements. Let's consider these next.

Business Vision/Mission Statement

When you start a business, you are full of conviction and purpose. You believe in what you are starting and want to stick to your values. You are committed to the mission of your business. You want to have this feeling and continue it each day. With a compelling vision and clear, worthwhile mission, you will not only inspire your business, but you'll also be able to keep your employees dedicated as well.

You can do this by creating strong mission and vision statements. These statements are meant to motivate and clearly express intent when communicating with anyone within your business. They also tell your customers, suppliers, and media what the purpose of your business is. Let's look at how you can create these statements.

Purpose

The mission and vision statements have two distinct jobs. Mission statements are used to define the purpose and primary objectives of the organization. These statements are worded in the present tense and explain why your business exists, both to people within the business and outside it. Mission statements are often short, clear, and strong.

Vision statements will also define the purpose of your business, but they focus more on the aspirations and goals. These statements focus on being inspiring and uplifting. The vision statement also doesn't change even if the strategy of the business changes.

Creating a Mission Statement

The first thing you want to do is develop a winning idea or a unique selling position (USP). This can be an approach or an idea that makes your business stand out from the competition. It is the reason why people should come to you rather than going to your competitors.

The next step is to make a short list of how you will measure success for this idea. In short, how will you know when you've reached your goal? You don't need exact figures, but you should have a general idea of what success is, so you know once you've reached it. Combine your idea from step one with general success measures into a measurable goal. Refine the wording until you have a concise statement that expresses your ideas, measures, and desired outcome.

This statement should be written in the present tense. It should be short and simple, written in clear language free of any "jargon." While the language needs to be inspiring, you shouldn't simply use adjectives to have it "sound better."

Creating a Vision Statement

Once you have a mission statement, you can focus on writing your vision statement. The vision statement is where you put the human value into the mission. How does your business impact others' lives?

You need to identify what you and anyone else going into business with you value most about your business and how you will achieve your mission statement. Then break this down into values that you want your business to have. Some popular options include excellence, integrity, teamwork, originality, equality, honesty, freedom, service, and strength. If you have a hard time determining values, then talk to others and what they think your business should stand for.

Next, combine your mission and values and polish your words into an inspiring statement that energizes people both inside and outside your business. The statement should be broad and timeless while explaining to others why people in your business do what they do.

Both your mission and vision statements need to be concise and inspiring while clearly communicating the direction and values of your business. These statements are powerful explanations of your intentions and can motivate you and your employees to have a vision for the future of the business. Once you have these two statements prepared, then you can move on to one of the most important business documents, the business plan.

The Business Plan

The business plan is the single most important document you can have when starting a business. It provides a roadmap to starting your business while also laying out your plan for growing and expanding your business. It is needed for you to be able to seek financing or assistance when starting your business. If you aren't comfortable putting together this document yourself, be sure to seek help for any areas that you aren't comfortable with. Let's consider the segments you need to put together for a successful and well laid out business plan.

Executive Summary

Discuss what your facility will offer and what it has that will make it stand out from the competition.

- Are you more of a campground with basic sites for RVs, or do you offer luxury RV sites with a number of recreational activities?

- What services does your facility offer to guests and potentially the community?

- What research and statistics show that you're facility is in the right area to overcome the competition and do something unique?

- Is there a way that your facility will help support the local community?

- What is the working environment you'll provide for employees?

- How is the business going to owned, managed, and run?

- What is the experience of those who are in charge of the business?

All of this will need to be covered at the start of your business plan.

Services and Amenities

Provide a list of the services and amenities that your business will offer. Consider some of the following examples:

- Offer campgrounds

- Offer overnight recreational camping

- Offers travel trailer and caravan campsites

- Offers wilderness camps

- Has a food and drink court

- Has a restaurant

- Has an ice cream shop

Basically, you'll want to list anything that is related to the operation of your facility and is available to your guests.

Mission and Vision Statement

Here you will write down the vision statement you came up with for your company. Follow it up by statement the mission statement for your company. The last portion will be to state how you will contribute to the local communities and what benefits your facility will bring to the area.

Business Structure

What is the goal of your business, and how will your business structure help you achieve your goals? What type of employees do you plan to hire? How will your employees help you build your business into what you want to achieve? What profit-sharing arrangement will be available for the senior management staff? List all the potential positions that will be found in your facility, such as the following:

- Chief Executive Officer (CEO)

- Facility Manager

- Accountant

- Marketing and Sales Officer

- Recreational Vehicle Park Safety Instructor and/or Assistant

- Customer Care Executives

- Cleaners

Job Roles and Responsibilities

In this same section, you'll also want to describe what the roles and responsibilities will be for each member of the facility. Consider some of the following examples:

Chief Executive Officer (CEO) -

- Responsible for recruiting, selecting, orienting, training, coaching, counseling, and disciplining managers.

- Communicates values, strategies, and objectives for the company.

- Assigns accountabilities.

- Plans, monitors, and appraises job results.

- Develops incentives.

- Develops a system for offering information and opinions.

- Provides educational opportunities.

- Creates, communicates, and implements anything related to the vision, mission, and overall direction of the company.

- Responsible for fixing prices and signing business deals.

- Provides for the direction of the business.

- Signs checks and documents on behalf of the company.

- Evaluates the overall success of the business.

- Responsible for staff induction for new team members.

Facility Manager -

- Responsible for the operation and management of the facility.

- Makes sure the facility is in a top position at all times.

- Manages any food and beverage services.

- Oversees membership and registration services.

- Responsible for equipment rentals and sales services.

- Handles all aspects of facility operation.

Accountant -

- Prepares financial reports, budgets, and financial statements for the business.

- Provides management with financial analyses, development budgets, and accounting reports.

- Analyzes the financial feasibility for proposed complex projects.

- Does market research in order to forecast trends and business conditions.

- Responsible for financial forecasting and risk analysis.

- Responsible for cash management, ledger accounting, and financial reporting.

- Develops and manages financial systems and policies.

- Administers payrolls.

- Ensures all compliance with tax legislation.

- Handles financial transactions for the business.

- Serves as an internal auditor.

Marketing and Sales Officer -

- Identifies, prioritizes, and reaches out to both new clients and business opportunities.

- Looks for development opportunities and follows up on development leads and contacts.

- Helps with the structuring and financing of the project while assuring its completion.

- Writes proposal documents, negotiates fees, and rates in line with the business policy.

- Handles business research, market surveys, and feasibility studies.

- Oversees implementation, advocates for customer needs, and communicates with clients.

- Develops, executes, and evaluates plans for expanding sales.

- Documents customer contact and information.

- Represents the business in strategic meetings.

- Helps to grow the business and increase sales.

Recreational Vehicle Park Safety Instructor and/or Assistant -

- Ensures guests follow safety measures when they use recreational vehicles.

- Responsible for all amusement and recreation services.

- Handles registration for any on-site tournaments or matches.

- Handles and provides instruction for services available at the facility.

Customer Care Executives -

- Welcomes guests in person or on the phone.

- Answers and directs all inquiries.

- Provides personalized customer service of the highest level to clients through all communication methods.

- On the phone, attempts to build a client's interest in the business' products and/or services.

- Manages administrative duties assigned by management.

- Stays informed on organization products to help clients as needed.

Cleaners -

- Responsible for cleaning all areas in and around the facility.

- Cleans up after guests and work areas.

- Washes dishes in food areas as needed.

- Ensures proper supply and stock of all necessary items.

- Handles all duties assigned by the manager.

SWOT Analysis

In this area, you will show that you've done your research into the competition in your area as well as the business organization in general. How will your business plan to break even, and how soon do you foresee this happening? You will do this by writing four different sections.

Strengths

What strengths and advantages does your facility offer? Are you centrally located near a populated area or near a major attraction? Will you offer membership packages to increase business? Are you in a high traffic area and offer visibility to increase overnight stays? Make sure you cover your strengths in detail and have research to back up these strengths.

Weakness

There are always going to be weaknesses when starting a business, and you want to be open about them when discussing them here. Perhaps you are a new business without the necessary capital to compete with other facilities in the area. Maybe you can only accommodate certain types of RV rigs. Whatever your weaknesses are, list them here and provide possible solutions and timelines for resolution here.

Opportunities

What opportunities can you take advantage of in your area? Are you near a dense population area? This is similar to the strengths, but it is more about the opportunities in your area that you can use to grow strengths for your facility.

Threats

What are some likely threats your facility will face when getting started? Are there government or local policies that you need to overcome? What are the demographic factors? Is the projected economy going to present problems? Are there any potential impacts on your projected business future that need to be discussed?

Market Analysis

What are the recent market trends for the RV park industry? Have people been directed more towards recreational activities? Do consumer trends lean more towards healthy living and lifestyles? What will make guests more likely to come to your facility than others? What are the current trends within the industry that show you are well-positioned and equipped to be successful? What plans do you have in place to constantly keep a revenue stream coming into your business even if the market trends are down? What do you plan for the growth of your business? Will you add services or offer programs to increase traffic to your facility?

Target Market

While the RV park industry often focuses on people from different backgrounds, you are still going to want to define a target market. There are a number of reasons why people will choose to visit or register at an RV park, and it is these reasons that influence marketing and business trends. There are three various groups you can consider when defining your target market.

First is families who want to have time to hang out and bond together. The second group is schools that are looking for a place to take children for outdoor activities. Lastly, there are clubs and organizations that focus on outdoor activities and recreation. In this section of your business plan, you want to list exactly which categories of people you are looking to attract to your facility.

Competitive Advantage

The RV park industry is certainly prolific and, in some areas, can even be highly competitive. Guests will come to your facility if they know you can successfully provide them what they want, which is often to enjoy the great outdoors. While you have been discussing your advantages throughout the business plan, this area is to showcase what makes you stand out from the competition.

Perhaps you have a highly qualified team that is better at giving guests what they need. Or maybe you will be offering a membership package that is more attractive than the competition. Another thing might be the way you treat your employees makes it more possible to hire the right people to adequately provide for guests.

Sales and Marketing Strategy

Your marketing strategies should be focused on achieving a specific objective that supports the overall goals of your business. Marketing is focused on creating new market channels, increasing sales, and increasing your share of the market. To do this, you may need to improve your facility or services to gain new guests or get old ones to return.

In this section of your business plan, you will define your marketing strategies. It is important to be consistent with a mix of marketing strategies that show focus on product improvement, promotion, and price. Again you should briefly mention what it is about your facility that stands out from the competition and how you can showcase this in your marketing and sales plan. Some ideas for what to put in this section include the following:

- Open our facility with a grand opening ceremony.

- Advertise our facility in national dailies and local media.

- Promote our facility online through an official website and all social media platforms.

- Sending out introductory letters with promotional materials to organizations, schools, and households within a specific area near our facility.

- Place promotional materials in key public areas to possibly direct traffic to the facility.

- Maintaining a great and impressive first impression to help get return customers.

- Use a direct mailing coupon marketing approach.

- Position signs and banners in strategic places near the facility.

- Develop a loyalty plan that helps to reward consistent guests.

- Engage in local community events in order to promote awareness for your facility.

Sources of Income

Here you want to summarize what you will do to attract both individual and group guests on a regular basis and where your sources of income will come from. Some examples include the following:

- Operating campgrounds and RV sites.

- Operating wilderness camps.

- Offering food and drink through a restaurant and/or food court.

- Other related facility operations.

Sales Forecast

Based on your feasibility studies and assumptions from the industry, you want to put together a sales forecast. All your statistics should be at least one year old to show a pattern in consumer spending. If you aren't comfortable with this section, it can be a good idea to have an accountant put it together for you. It should overall look something like the following:

- First Fiscal Year - $250,000

- Second Fiscal Year - $400,000

- Third Fiscal Year - $800,000

Pricing Strategy

Here you will state what your pricing strategy will be. Often it is based on what is obtainable within the industry. You won't charge more unless it is for premium and/or customized services. You also won't charge less than your competitors. However, you can also include discount services to reward loyal customers or when some refers people to your facility. The prices should always be the same as the open market.

Payment Options

Here you simply need to list what payment options you will have available for guests. Such as:

- Bank transfer

- Cash

- Credit cards

- Check

- Mobile money transfer

- Bank draft

Startup Budget

When setting up any business, the cost depends on your approach and the scale you are trying to undertake. For example, if you plan to lease the land, then you'll need a lot of capital. Basically, this also means that your start-up budget can be either high or low, depending on your goals, vision, and aspirations. The tools and equipment are nearly the same anywhere. In this section, you want to provide a detailed cost analysis for starting your facility. It should look something like the following:

- Registering the business - $750

- Licenses and permits - $1,500

- Marketing and promotions expenses - $5,000

- Hiring a business consultant - $1,000

- Insurance premium - $30,000

- Cost of software - $3,000

- Cost for leasing the land - $200,000

- Remodeling and equipping the facility - $100,000

- Phone and utility deposits - $3,000

- Three months operational costs - $100,000

- Start-up inventory - $5,000

- Furniture and equipment costs - $10,000

- Website production and launch - $500

- Grand opening party - $1,000

- Miscellaneous costs - $5,000

Generating Startup Capital

Here you'll discuss and list your major sources for start-up capital. Are you going to get your capital from personal savings and sales of stocks? Perhaps you'll be borrowing from extended family and friends? Is the majority of your financing going to come from a bank loan?

If you already have funds in place, then state how much you have already. Also, be specific on where these funds come from. Also, be clear with how much money you still need to raise or what you are asking for if you are presenting the business plan to a financial institution.

Sustainability and Expansion Strategy

The future of any RV facility is in loyal customers. This is linked to everything from employees to investment strategy and business structure. If any single factor is missing from a business, then there won't be a loyal customer base, and it won't be long before the business needs to close. One of the biggest goals for your business is to survive off your cash flow without needing to get additional financing from an external source once the business is running. In this section, you need to discuss in detail how you plan to gain and keep loyal customers. End your business plan by summarizing how you plan to expand your business once it becomes successful.

Other Paperwork Housekeeping

With a strong business plan in place, you can use it to seek assistance for the start-up. Even if you are already set to get your business running, the business plan can provide you with a great road map to keeping the operation of your business on track. After you've finished this, you can move on to the next step in starting your business, which is setting up a legal entity to operate under.

Register as a Legal Entity

When it comes to starting an RV facility, you generally have three options for choosing a legal entity:

1. General Partnership

2. Limited Liability Company (LLC)

3. Sole Proprietorship

In general, a sole proprietorship can be an ideal business model for a small RV facility if you only need moderate start-up capital. However, most prefer an LLC for many obvious reasons. If you plan to grow your business to include facilities throughout the United States and/or Canada, then choosing a sole proprietorship isn't the right option. In these situations, an LLC or general partnership is a better idea.

Starting an LLC is also a great idea because it protects you from personal liability. This means that if someone goes wrong in the course of operating the business, then only the money you invested in the business will be at risk. With a sole proprietorship or a general partnership, this isn't the case. An LLC is also simpler and more flexible when it comes to operation, and you won't need to set up a board of directors, shareholder meetings, or other formalities of a managerial nature.

These are just a few of the main things to consider when choosing a legal entity for your RV facility. Some other things that you'll want to consider include limitation of personal liability, ease of transferability, admission of new owners, investors' expectations, and taxes. Your best option is to start as an LLC and then convert to a 'C' Corporation or an 'S' Corporation if needed should you choose to take your business public. Once you have a legal entity in place, you should focus on getting an EIN.

Obtain an EIN

An EIN or Employer Identification Number is issued for the purpose of tax administration and is not intended for participation in other activities such as a tax lien auction or sale. You should make sure your organization is formed legally before you apply for an EIN. There are three simple steps involved in getting your EIN and should be able to be done within a day.

First, you need to determine your eligibility. If your business is located in the United States or one of its Territories, then you can apply for an EIN online. The person who is applying for the EIN needs to have a valid Taxpayer Identification Number. The responsible party for an EIN needs to be the one who owns or controls the entity or business or at least someone who exercises ultimate control over the business. The responsible party needs to be an individual and not an entity.

The second step is to put together the online application. Simply complete the application in one session since you won't be able to save it and return later. The session will also expire after 15 minutes of inactivity, and you'll need to re-start.

The last step is to simply submit your application. If all validations are correct, you'll get an EIN immediately after completing the application. You will then be able to download, save, and print your confirmation notice.

Open a Business Bank Account

Once you have an EIN, you can open a business bank account and credit card. This should be done in order to accept or spend money as a business. Having a separate business bank account will help you to stay legally compliant and protected while also having benefits for your employees and customers.

Benefits of a Business Bank Account

Common business accounts include a checking account, savings account, credit card, and a merchant services account. A merchant services account will allow you to accept credit and debit card payments from guests. A business bank account can be opened once you have an EIN. Most business accounts will have benefits that you don't get with a standard personal bank account. Consider some of the benefits you will receive.

With business banking, you get limited personal liability protection by having your business funds separate from your personal funds. With merchant services, you also have purchase protection for guests and ensure that personal information is secured.

A business account also offers the benefit of professionalism. Guests can pay with a credit card and make checks out to a business rather than to an individual. You'll also be able to authorize employees to handle routine banking tasks for the business.

A business bank account will help you to be prepared. Most business banking comes with the option of opening a line of credit for the business. This can be used if you experience an emergency or if you need to purchase new and expensive equipment for your facility.

Lastly, a business bank account gives you purchasing power. Credit card accounts can help you to make large purchases for start-up purposes. This will also help to increase the credit history for your business.

Finding an Account

Some people choose to open a business account at the same bank where they have a personal account. However, you should keep in mind that the rates, fees, and options vary between banks. This means you should shop around and ensure you are finding the lowest fees and best benefits before opening a bank account. Consider the following when choosing where to open a business bank account:

- Introductory offers

- Interest rates for checking and savings

- Interest rates for lines of credit

- Transaction fees

- Early termination fees

- Minimum account balance fees

When it comes to open a merchant services account you'll also want to consider the following:

- The discount rate or the percentage charged for every transaction processed.

- The transaction fees or the amount charged for each credit card transaction.

- Address Verification Service (AVS) fees.

- ACH daily batch fees that are charged when you settle credit card transactions for a day.

- Monthly minimum fees charged when a business doesn't mean minimum required transactions.

A popular alternative to merchant services accounts that are gaining in popularity is using payment processing companies. These will sometimes offer extra functionality, such as accessories that allow you to use your phone to accept payments by credit card. The fee categories you should consider are similar to those of a merchant services account fees. If there is a payment processor you like, then keep in mind that you'll still need to link it to a business checking account in order to receive payments.

What You Need to Open an Account

Once you've chosen a bank, then you can open your account. All you need to do to start the process is to go online or head to a local branch. Some of the most common documents you'll need when opening a business account include the following:

- EIN Number

- Business formation documents

- Ownership agreements

- Business license

From here, you should focus on getting your licenses and permits in order. Let's consider what is involved in this step.

Business License and Permits

Most new businesses will need some combination of licenses and permits from both federal and state agencies in order to get started. The actual requirements and fees will depend on your business activities, location, and government rules. Let's look at these requirements in general.

Federal Licenses and Permits

If any of your facility activities are regulated by a federal agency, then you'll need to contact that agency to see if there are any associated federal licenses and/or permits that you need to apply for. The requirements and fees will depend on the activity and the agency that is issuing the permit or license. It is best to check with the agency responsible for the most detailed information.

State Licenses and Permits

Licenses and permits can also vary by state, county, or city. This will depend largely on your facility location, but can also be determined by your activities. States tend to have a broader range of regulations for activities than the federal government. Some common activities include auctions, construction, farming, plumbing, restaurants, retail, and vending machines.

After a set period of time, some licenses and permits will expire. Be sure you keep track of when you need to renew these since it is often easier to do the renewal process than it is to have to apply for a new one. Take the time to research the licenses and permits required in your area. You can visit your state's website or contact the county controller for the most accurate information.

Insurance and Bonds

Having business insurance will protect you from unexpected costs. Accidents, natural disasters, and lawsuits could all potentially shut down your business if you don't have the proper insurance coverage. Let's consider what level of coverage you need.

The protection you get from a business structure such as an LLC only protects your personal property from things like a lawsuit, and even this is limited protection. You can fill this gap with proper business insurance so that your personal and business assets are fully protected from any potentially unexpected occurrences.

In some areas, you may be required to purchase a specific type or level of business insurance. The federal government requires all businesses that hire employees to have workers' compensation, unemployment, and disability insurance. Some states will also require additional insurance. The laws will vary by state, and you can contact your state for information on just what level of insurance you are required to have.

Common Types of Business Insurance

After purchasing the required insurance, you can also choose to get additional insurance to help cover other business risks. The general rule is that you should insure against anything that you can't pay for on your own. If you need help, you can speak with an insurance agent about the best coverage for your business and compare plans to get you the best terms and prices. However, the six most common forms of business insurance you may want to consider are the following.

General Liability Insurance

This insurance can be for any business. It protects against financial loss that results from bodily injury, property damage, medical expenses, libel, slander, defending lawsuits, and settlement bonds or judgments.

Product Liability Insurance

Ideal for businesses that manufacture, wholesale, distribute, and retail products. This insurance protects against financial loss as a result of defective products that result in bodily harm or injury.

Professional Liability Insurance

Ideal for businesses that provide services to customers. It protects against financial loss that comes from malpractice, errors, and negligence.

Commercial Property Insurance

A good idea for businesses with a large amount of property and physical assets. It protects the business against loss and damage to company property as a result of a wide range of events, including fire, smoke, wind, hail storms, civil disobedience, and vandalism.

Home-Based Business Insurance

Often only needed for businesses that are run out of a personal home. The coverage is added to homeowner's insurance as a rider and helps protect for a small amount of equipment and liability coverage from third-party injuries.

Business Owner's Policy

Most small businesses benefit from this coverage, but especially those with a home-based business. It is an insurance package that combines all of the main coverage options into a single bundle. It helps simplify the purchase process and helps save some money.

Buying Business Insurance

There are four main steps to take when it comes to purchasing your business insurance. The first step is to assess your risks. Consider what types of accidents, natural disasters, or lawsuits that can potentially impact your business. If you need help choosing and assessing your risks, then you can check with the National Federation of Independent Businesses (NFIB).

The second step is to look for a reputable licensed agent. A commercial insurance agent can help you find the policy that best meets your needs. Insurance agents typically receive commissions from insurance companies to sell policies, so it is important you choose a licensed agent carefully.

Next, you want to shop around for the best policy. Benefits and prices can vary greatly between companies. Be sure to compare rates, terms, and benefits from several different agents before making a final decision.

Lastly, make sure you reassess your insurance needs every year. As a business grows, the liabilities may change. If you have either expanded or purchased new equipment, then you should talk with your insurance agent to see if your insurance coverage is affected.

Marketing and Advertising

The fact that it is easy to start an RV facility means that there are more competitors, no matter where your facility is located. This means you need to make yourself stand out on the market both in your local community, city, state, and even country. When it comes to set up marketing and advertising strategies for your facility, you need to consider a variety of options.

Consider some of the following tips to help you market and advertise your business for maximum potential:

- Send out introduction letters with promotional materials such as brochures to organizations, clubs, schools, and households in your area that may be interested in the services offered at your facility.

- Have a grand opening ceremony at your facility in order to get the attention of nearby residents who are likely to be your first potential guests.

- Have flyers and business cards made in order to leave them in offices, libraries, and any public facility that potential guests may frequent.

- Use handbills or other materials to create awareness and provide directions to your park if you aren't on the main route.

- Visit community events and roadshows that feature your target audience in order to market your services.

- Advertise in local media, including newspapers, TV, and radio.

- List your business in the yellow pages.

- Use the internet to promote your facility to farther areas for those looking to travel to your area.

- Utilize direct marketing and sales.

- Encourage guests to use word of mouth marketing to refer new guests to your facility.

- Join the local chamber of commerce and partner with nearby industries in order to network and market your facility.

In addition to general marketing and advertising, it is also important that you work to boost your brand awareness and create a strong identity for your business. This is especially important if you plan to eventually expand your business beyond the local area. In order to continue to appeal to your target audience, you need to be consistent in promoting brand awareness. Developing an identity is key to building a profitable business.

There are several platforms you can utilize in order to boost your brand and develop a strong corporate identity, such as the following:

- Advertise in print and electronic media.

- Sponsor community events.

- Use all social media platforms.

- Consider billboards.

- Engage in roadshows.

- Contact organizations that may want to use your facility for events.

- Get listed in local directories.

- Have an official website and pull in as much traffic as possible.

- Have employees wear branded uniforms and have all vehicles marked with the company logo.

- Position your logo in as many places as possible throughout the facility.

Since an RV park not only relies on local business but also traveling individuals, you need to focus on your far-reaching marketing efforts. This means reaching potential guests from around the world who are looking for a vacation destination and need a reason to choose you. One great option that is often overlooked is the RV online directory.

It isn't exactly known how many RV destinations are chosen in advance versus those that are decided on while driving down the road. There are probably some that prefer the peace of mind of having reservations in advance with a planned trip. Guests traveling from a farther distance or at busier times of the year are more likely to do their research and set reservations in advance. For this reason, it can be beneficial to have your facility listed in an RV directory.

Most RVers will travel with at least one major print directory. Often people won't have access to a facility's website while traveling on the road. Often the information in a directory listing will provide all the information a traveler needs to make a decision about which park to stay at. Consider some important things to include in your directory listing.

Make sure a directory adequately lists the elements of your park. This includes a listing of amenities, number of sites, interior road surface, site spacing, last year's prices, and other important information that helps individuals choose an RV facility.

In addition, make sure the directory listing has easy to understand directions to your park. Whether your park is right off the main road or a bit harder to reach, make sure your directions are as simple and clear as possible.

If you have any special amenities or activities that other parks in your area don't offer, highlight them in your directory listing.

Doing these things will help you get noticed far and wide, bringing in as many potential guests as possible. The next step to consider in operating your RV facility is to start hiring the right employees and having the right level of staffing.

Employees

Your employees are responsible for the health and safety of all guests. They need to stick with their job duties and maintain performance standards in order to provide the best possible guest experience. In addition, employees are responsible for sustainability efforts that will have a positive impact on the facility. For all these reasons and more, you want to hire and keep the best possible employees for your facility. There are a few ways to do this. First, let's look at how many employees you should be hiring.

How Many Employees to Hire

In addition to finances, there are a few things to decide when determining how many employees to hire. If you are going to be starting a large scale RV facility then you need to have the following positions at a minimum:

- Chief Operating Officer

- Marketing and Sales Executive

- Accountant

- Recreational Vehicle Park Safety Officer/Assistant

- Human Resources and Administration Manager

- Facility Manager

- Customer Services Officer

- Security Guards

- Cleaners

A medium to large scale RV facility is going to need a minimum of 10 to 15 staff members in order to operate effectively.

Employee Skills

Just as you need specific skills and interests to start an RV facility, your employees need to have a specific skill set in order to be successful and strong employees that help to grow your business. There are four main traits you should look for when choosing and hiring employees.

First, you want employees with good interpersonal skills. The RV facility is a part of the hospitality industry, so you want employees that are people persons. You want employees who will cater to the needs of guests and solve any issues that may come up with a person's stay.

Also, an RV park employee should be an outdoor person. They are often going to be out in nature more than behind a desk. Most routine tasks will occur outside. Plus, it will make it easier to understand and appreciate the lifestyle of your guests.

Third, the employee should be an autonomous leader. You can't be there all the time as an owner. Therefore, employees should be able to self-manage on their own if needed. Yet they should also know when is the right time to get the owner of the facility involved.

Lastly, look for employees with prior experience and/or education. Previous experience in any camp-like job or having an education in the hospitality sector can be a big plus. This experience and knowledge can help with managing daily operations as well as facing any challenges that come along the way.

Knowing what to look for in an employee is only the first step in the hiring process. From there, you need to have an employment application process to help narrow down potential applicants.

The Job Application

A job application is a document that you can use as an employer to collect information from people who are applying for a position at your RV facility. It provides you with basic information about the potential employee.

What Can't Be Asked

It is important to remember that an application can't ask for any of the following:

- Race

- Color

- Religion

- Gender Identity

- Sexual Orientation

- Pregnancy

- National Origin

- If an applicant is over the age of 40

- Disability

- Genetic Information

The hiring process isn't an easy one, and you need to find the right individual who is going to benefit your business. You also have to put a lot of time and effort into training and retaining employees, so you want to hire the right one. A job application can help you screen applicants and interview only those who fit your needs the best. You should always use a job application since it gives you a good first impression of the potential employee. Let's look at the components that should be on a job application.

Components of a Job Application

Personal Information -

- Full legal name and any prior names.

- Current address.

- Mailing address if different from a residential address.

- Date of Birth.

- Telephone number(s).

- Email address.

- Verification of the applicant's eligibility to work.

- Start date requested by the applicant.

Employment History -

- There should be spaces for three to five entries with requests for the following information:

    ☐ Dates of employment with the most recent job first.

    ☐ Company name and address.

☐ Job title.

☐ Summary of duties.

☐ Reason for leaving.

☐ Supervisor information.

Other Information -

- Has the applicant ever been convicted of a crime? Leave room for an explanation.

- Is the applicant a veteran? Leave room for duty and training.

Education -

There should be space for high school, college, business/technical school, and other specialized training. Leave enough room in all categories in case there are multiple schools.

Training and Special Skills -

You can decide whether or not to include this area. Perhaps your potential employee knows CPR or other useful skills that could place them ahead of other applicants. If this is the case, then leave this area on the application.

Contacts -

The standard is to ask for three references. They can be either personal or professional references, but can't be related to the applicant. Encourage a combination of personal and professional references so you can have a well-rounded view of the individual.

Do You Need an Application?

While not a requirement, it is generally advisable to have and use applications. The application is an important tool to help you quickly screen potential employees and determine who is the best option. The application will make the initial review of an applicant a fair process. It offers a standard and easy to read format. Also, reviewing an application will often take less time than a resume.

Legal Considerations

If you need to hire employees, then you need to create a job application. Creating an application can actually be a more complex process than you might think. There are some legal considerations to take into account when creating an application. Through the application, you are basically interacting with a stranger, and federal as well as state laws determine what you can and can't ask on an application. So while you want to use the application to get specific information, you need to make sure you carefully write your application. Keep the following in mind and hire a labor law attorney if needed.

Be Obvious

When writing a legal document, this can often be the most artful part. The terms of an application, dictate the nature of the action they will perform.

- Have a statement on the application that your business is an "Equal Opportunity Employer." Omitting this statement means that denied applicants have the opportunity to file a complaint.

- Make sure the application states that submitting an application is not a guarantee of employment. Without this, you may be forced to hire someone who isn't a good fit or is unqualified for the position.

- Avoid using any adjectives that can be interpreted as preferential at any point in the hiring process. This means avoiding any descriptors that imply or question any of the areas discussed at the beginning. Also, make sure you include a line that states you won't discriminate based on these terms.

Local Obligations

Your application should also comply with any state and municipal regulations. Research your local laws when it comes to employment. An easier option may be to discuss it with an attorney.

Generic Information

Again you can't ask for information related to ethnicity, race, gender, religion, parenting, or marital status. You should also avoid the subject of social or political affiliations. Otherwise, your business may appear to be discriminating.

Writing an application isn't the easiest, so if needed, ask for help. There are also templates online you can use if you need help. Once you have an application and begin to use them, then you can move on to the interview process.

How to Conduct Interviews

A crucial part of the hiring process is to learn how to conduct an interview and become a good interviewer. The best job interview will give the interviewee a chance to learn about the company while providing the interviewer with the chance to learn about the potential employee. An effective job interview will help you with the process of hiring the best employee, but you'll need to prepare ahead of time and consider your needs so you can guide the interview. Let's look at how you can perform an excellent interview.

What is the Job Interview?

Knowing how to interview someone is important. When you interview properly, you will be able to better understand the contents of the application and resume. The questions you ask will also allow you to measure a potential employee's ability to think quickly, describe work scenarios, and sometimes perform unexpected work tasks. The interview is also a great way to compare applicants and choose the one that best fits the needs.

Conducting a Job Interview

Each question asked during a job interview needs to be intentional, so you need to make sure you prepare ahead of time. Let's look at the steps you should take to prepare for and conduct an interview.

Preparation

Prepare for the interview process by evaluating the position you are hiring for and what it will do for the company. Compare these needs with the expected educational, skills, and experience requirements of the ideal candidate. Organize these requirements into a list and use them to guide you when creating interview questions.

The STAR Process

A common technique that is used in the interview process is known as the STAR method. This stands for:

- Situation - Describe a situation or challenge faced.

- Task - Describe the task or requirement.

- Action - Describe the action taken to overcome the situation.

- Result - Describe the result or the outcome of the action.

This method is often used by interviewees when you ask them behavioral questions. These questions ask interviewees to describe a time when they used specific skills or overcame a challenge. This method can be used to rate the answers or to create follow-up questions or get new information from an answer to better understand previous experience levels.

Describe the Company and Position

Start the interview by introducing yourself and discussing what position you are looking to fill. Give a brief background of the company and how the position fits into the objectives and goals of the company. This allows the interviewee a chance to understand what is expected of them and the responsibilities they may be faced with if they get the position.

Explain the Interview Process

Tell the interviewee what they can expect to experience during the interview process. This includes the format, expected time, and whether or not they will be required to perform work-related tasks. This allows the interview to be organized and provides clear objectives and expectations for all parties involved.

Learn About Career Goals

Before you get into role-specific questions, it can be a good idea to under the career goals of the interviewee. Ask general questions about their professional interests and why they applied for the position. This allows you to understand their expectations when it comes to professional development and promotions. It also allows you to assess how much they understand about your company and the open position.

Ask Position-Specific Questions

Once you know the interviewee's career goals, you can now start asking position-specific questions. You should come up with a list of intended questions in advance. If you plan to interview multiple people, then you may also want to establish a way to grade each individual. This can be based on their confidence and poise when answering, their ability to clearly answer, and whether or not they addressed all parts of the questions. You can also choose to develop a more analytical grading if there are more technical questions.

Follow Up Questions

Use follow up questions to gather more information about a person's experience. You may not be able to get some information from direct questions, but by asking a person to describe an experience further can give you more insight into their experience. If needed, you should always be ready to expand on a question and use your list of questions as a guide rather than a hard and fast plan.

Entertain Interviewee Questions

The best employment agreement benefits both the interviewee as well as the interviewer. Provide time for the interviewee to ask questions about the position or the company. This allows the interviewee to evaluate if the position is the right fit for them, and it allows you to measure their interest and understanding of your company.

Describe Next Steps

At the end of the interview, you should inform the candidate about what they can expect next. At this time, you can also offer them feedback on the interview. Provide them with an intended timeline for filling the position, when they can expect a response and when they may be expected to start employment.

Once you've hired an employee, you need to collect certain information from them and maintain certain records. This will be the next area to consider.

Employee Records

Once you hire an employee, you'll need to maintain records as an employer. There are four employee record files you need to maintain as an employer. Let's look at each of these.

Personnel Files

Each employee should have a personnel file maintained. These files often contain confidential documents and are managed and maintained by a human resources officer. Personnel files are the main records for an employee that are utilized by the employer, employee, and manager.

The personnel file typically includes the employment application, a family emergency contact form, documented disciplinary action history, a resume, the employee handbook receipt sign off, at-will employer sign off sheets, the periodic appraisal, job evaluation or performance development plan, training certificates, and attendance evidence, and current personal contact information.

Not all the same files will be in each personnel file. Documentation of an employee's performance wouldn't be in a personnel file unless it resulted in disciplinary action, an award, or other sign of outstanding achievement. Everyday performance notes stay in the manager's file to track performance, goals, and contributions by employees.

Payroll Files

These contain a history of the employee's jobs, departments, compensation changes, garnishments, loans, and other information key to paying an employee and keeping a copy. The payroll file will also contain forms such as the W-2, W-4, and social security withholding documents. Employee benefits information and permission to withdraw payments from the paycheck should also be included.

Medical Files

An employer should also maintain an employee medical file. The records in this file should be available to no one other than the human resources officer and the employee. The medical file should contain doctor's notes, FMLA application paperwork, drug test information, required physical information, and other documentation that relates to an employee or their family's medical health. Because of the confidentiality of these records, they should have the highest degree of safe storage and confidentiality. They should be kept in locked file drawers in a room that is not accessible to employees other than designated staff.

I-9 Files

These are maintained for all employees in a file that is separate from other employee records. This is to maintain employee confidentiality from government officials and others who are authorized to review employee I-9s. The I-9 form is a document that is designed to ensure that a newly hired employee is legally able to work in the United States.

Tips and Advice for Being a Good Employer

Some companies are known for lavish employee perks, but being a good employer means more than offering perks. And if you're a small business, you may not be able to compete with the larger companies when it comes to perks and benefits. Rather focus on creating a culture that employees will feel valued in so they will be invested in helping your business stay successful. If you work to be a good employer, then you reduce employee stress and improve your business. Let's look at six things you can do to be a good employer.

Communication

You should focus on open and honest communication. Keep your employees informed on what is going on with the business. Explain the mission as well as short and long term goals. Regularly keep them updated on how the business is going. This will help your employees feel trusted and secure, so they are more likely to identify with the mission and values of the company.

Flexibility

Employees don't appreciate a bunch of rules with no explanations. Most employees want some form of work-life balance, especially if they have a family. In fact, most employees say that the most stressful part of their job is juggling their work and personal lives. The best employers are those who are open to alternative arrangements like working from home part-time. When you send the message that you want employees to have a well-rounded life and trust them to work even when you're not there, then you'll improve your employees' lives.

Team Building

Employers who care about their business and its mission need to inspire their employees to feel the same. This will help make the workplace more pleasant for all. Great employers also view their employees as important members of the team who need to work together in order for the business to survive. As an employer, you should create a culture where your employees are proud of the business and want to see it succeed.

Give Feedback

Employees typically want an employer to give feedback so they can do their job better and continue to grow professionally. As an employer, you should tell your employees when they are doing a good job, but also provide them with regular advice on how to improve. Make sure the advice is framed in a positive way and not as a criticism.

Know How to Listen

The best employers know they don't have all the answers, so they will be open to ideas and insights from employees if it can improve the company. They will also listen to complaints and think it through before offering an empathetic and genuine response. Listen and respond to feedback to help your employees feel empowered.

Foster a Great Experience

Provide your employees with the right environment and tools. This could be anything from a comfortable break room to a mentorship program. Ask your employees for what they want and do your best to accommodate.

Becoming a great employer takes work, and it can be a struggle to do this while starting a business. But as if you show that you are making an effort, most employees will be satisfied. This will pay off in higher morale, lower turnover, and better productivity. You'll also have dedicated team members who work with you to make your business a long-term success.

Running an RV Park

Running an RV facility can be fun, but it can also be a lot of hard work. Consider the following tips and tricks to help you have success in running your RV facility. We'll discuss a few more ideas in a moment, but these are just some general overall tips to get you started.

Know the Industry

If you know nothing about owning an RV facility, then take the time to do some research or read a guide like this to get you more informed on the industry. It is important to become familiar with the consumer's point of view. While this may seem obvious, a lot of new owners fail to do this.

Spend a few weeks traveling in an RV and staying at some facilities in order to understand both sides of the issue.

Create a Community

Don't focus on long term guests only, but also consider short term guests with daily activities and community events. For example, you could host an ice cream social on July 4th. When you create a sense of community, then everyone will enjoy the atmosphere, and it will create memories associated with your facility. You can also foster a community sense with little amenities like a cup of coffee to people while they check-in or a postcard that they can send to family. Little things don't cost a lot, but can be a great benefit to your facility.

Learn the Basics

If you don't know much about things like electricity and plumbing in an RV, then take a class or two. You may be able to hire someone to handle these issues for you, but knowing the basics can save you in both time and money. Also, knowing the basics will keep guests happy since you will be able to offer them quick solutions.

Cleanliness is Important

Most guests are going to come to you from word of mouth from other guests who have stayed at your facility. This is why you want to maintain a clean and updated park. Without clean amenities like bathrooms and showers, you are quickly going to lose both short and long term guests.

Keep It Simple

Keep as much of the check-in and out process as streamlined as possible. This can make the difference between a good and a great experience. Check-in is the first interaction guests will have with your facility. This means more than the day they arrive, but also the time from when they book their reservation. Make the reservation process comfortable and easy as well.

Do It Right

If you are choosing to build your facility from scratch, then you need to do it with the right permits the first time. Not getting the right permits could easily cost you more later on down the line. Do the proper paperwork the first time, and things will go a lot smoother for you.

Marketing

You need to stay ahead of your competition in order to have success, and you can do this with correct marketing. The key is having a strong social media presence. We'll discuss more about this soon.

Adding Facilities

While marketing helps you to grow, adding facilities like a playground and outdoor sports can also help you stand out from the competition. This doesn't mean you need to pour money into your facility, you can easily find cheap improvements that add additional revenue. We've discussed a few already and will discuss some more in a moment. One easy area to add revenue is by holding special events during the seasons and holidays. Let's consider a few of those ideas.

Holding Special Events

Holiday events and seasonal events can be a great simple way of increasing revenue. Open these events to day guests as well as your RV guests. This can foster a sense of community and bring in people for the slower seasons. For example, during the fall season, which comes right after your peak season, you can keep guests coming with unique events such as the following:

- Host a luau complete with a pig roast.

- Have a fall festival and invite local vendors.

- Have a chili cook-off to fight off a cold day.

- Offer hayrides into the beautiful countryside.

- Celebrate veterans with a special dinner or picnic lunch.

At the same time, you can apply these ideas and others to holiday events. Even if you can't do something like a potluck on a holiday because of the weather, you can still do things for the holidays. If you close for the winter months, how about holding a social media contest for people to show off their winter RV decorations. It is a great way to create interest in your park and have people thinking of their future RV travel plans while you aren't in operation. Perhaps the most important part of running an RV facility is to provide top customer service. Let's look at how this can lead to the important long-term and returning RV traveler.

Customer Service

There are millions of RV owners in the United States, and when they travel, they need somewhere to stay. However, there are also plenty of places to choose from, and you need to stay out from the competition with excellent customer service if you expect these travelers to return each vacation and if you want them to refer other travelers to you. Let's look at how you can offer excellent customer service that is unforgettable.

You want to do more than simply please your guests, you want them to be excited about their stay. You can do this by over-delivering and providing more than they expected. This may sound like a lot of time and money, but there are only a few simple things you need to do to over-deliver for your guests. Consider what you can do.

Make sure your entry is attractive. This is your guests' first impression and sets the tone for how their stay will be at your facility. You should have attractive landscaping along with attractive signage. Everything should be well manicured and maintained.

Offer a warm and friendly greeting that is sincere. This also provides them with a strong first impression of what their stay is going to be like.

Offer travel advice. Most travelers are going to be new to the area, and you should provide them with a list of things to do based on their interests. You don't need to know all the details, but you should be able to provide the hours of operations and other information similar to a concierge at a hotel. Perhaps you can even have maps and flyers of nearby attractions so that your guests know where to go.

Lastly, make sure you check in with your guests once they've settled in and hooked up their utilities. It only takes a few minutes to stop in and make sure everything is going well. Your guests will appreciate this customer service, just like a waitress checks on you at a restaurant to ensure your meal is going well.

During a guest's stay, make sure you solve any problems. Studies have shown that customers who are unhappy and then made happy will be more loyal than people who have had no problems in the first place. This means you should try to solve all problems as soon as possible and to the customer's satisfaction. Along with customer service, the best thing you can do when running an RV facility is to keep up with social media.

Social Media

Social media is key to helping promote your park, and you should be active on all platforms as much as possible. There are five ways you can use social media platforms to benefit your facility. Let's consider those.

First, you can use social media to target your key audience with ads that showcase your facility. Social media platforms like Facebook allow you to be specific when targeting your ads. You can target those who live in your state, those who like camping, or those in a specific age range. If your focus is on families, then post about family events and target those who own RVs and have kids. This is a very effective way to increase guests to your facility.

Social media is a great platform for holding contests to get people talking about your facility. Have people share pictures and memories of their stay at your facility and then offer a prize such as a free weekend for the top entry. This is great to do in the slower season since it will get people talking about your facility and then potentially increase your guests once the travel season starts again.

Third, consider using sites like Instagram to focus on pictures of your facility and those who are enjoying their stay. This can be great when showcasing things like pets enjoying your facility. These days, pets are a huge draw for businesses, and people will certainly stay at a place that focuses on the four-legged family members.

Make sure you always ask for reviews on social media. People are likely to be members of at least one social media platform. Even if they don't review you on all the platforms, just one good review on any of the social media platforms will spread good word of mouth about your facility and potentially increase new guests.

Lastly, make sure there is a button that inspires your guests to act. Whether it is "Sign Up" or "Contact Us"; make sure there is a way for guests to get a hold of you and review your facility. This can also be a great way to get ideas for how to improve your park and guest experience.

Conclusion

As you can tell, there is a lot that goes into starting and running a successful RV facility. However, the benefits will make all the work barely noticeable. Once you're up and running, you can spend your days enjoying where you live and work. You'll be having a great lifestyle while helping others to have wonderful vacations and retired lives. So take what I've taught you here and you'll soon be seeing why I say this is the next best thing to being retired.

Made in the USA
Las Vegas, NV
21 September 2023